TALES OF A BOMBER COMMAND WAAF

With best wishes
from
Sylvia.

12. NOV. 02

First edition, published in 2002 by

WOODFIELD PUBLISHING
Woodfield House, Babsham Lane, Bognor Regis
West Sussex PO21 5EL, England.

ISBN 1-903953-24-3

Cover photograph: The Author with Bridget, a recent present from her father.

Tales of a
BOMBER COMMAND WAAF
(and her horse)

Sylvia (Bunty) Pickering

Woodfield

Dedicated to the memory of all aircrew, particularly those of No. 5 Group Bomber Command whose courage and stoical perseverance enabled them to fly night after night on raids against the enemy.

They were my heroes when I was eighteen. My tremendous admiration for them has not lessened now that I am seventy-nine years of age.

Sylvia Watts (née Pickering) 2002

All author's royalties from the sale of this book will be donated to RAF charities.

Contents

TALES OF A BOMBER COMMAND WAAF (*and her horse*)

With Compliments

Sylvia Watts and Dawn Bowskill

8 Musgraves Orchard,
Welton, Lincoln LN2 3NP

ACKNOWLEDGEMENTS

First of all I would like to thank Anthony Richards, Archivist, Department of Documents of the Imperial War Museum in London and Professor Peter H. Liddle MLitt, PhD, FRHistS Director of the Second World War Experience Centre, Leeds who both pleasantly surprised me by saying my memories and letters were worthy of retention when I sent them a sample. Thus encouraged I decided to write more about my life as a WAAF.

As a result of my past friendship with Tom Whiteley of 463 R.A.A.F. Squadron I was allowed to become an Hon. Member of 467/463 R.A.A.F. Squadron Association and there met the then Secretary, Ted Richardson. Ted found out for me about Roo's death and I then became in touch with Stan and Mary who met at the site. My ex-WAAF colleague Beryl Commin obtained for me other details about Roo and John Larder obtained Roo's "Gardening Map" and other details for me.

I am grateful for the piece from Sylvia Mandeville about witnessing the crash as a young evacuee and for Ann Mugridge's memories of R.A.F. Cottesmore. Also for Mike Garbett's gen that in the little snap of bombing up at O.T.U. it is for 250 lb. Bombs.

Mr. Tim Hart, Viscountess Campden, Sir David Davenport Handley and Mr. Ian McAlpine welcomed me to their lovely homes—the Old Hall, Market Overton, Exton Hall, Clipsham Hall and Peatling Parva Old Hall where once I had stayed and gave permission for Leslie, my husband, to take photographs for my book. Alice Gosling provided the excellent photos of the Grand Hotel—so pleased it still exists.

Beryl Williams, Sue Gates and Mrs. Joyce Pickering were kind enough to proof read the book—and the last named has continued to encourage me greatly whenever we meet. Thanks to Colin Bowskill for all his scanning magic and putting all Dawn and I have produced on C.D. ready for the publisher—a major task. To Dawn Bowskill my ever-grateful thanks for patiently giving so much of her time over the last twelve months to turn my "pipe dream" into reality—this book.

FOREWORD

It has been my enormous good fortune to have spent the last six years researching the history of the WAAF, and Sylvia and I first started corresponding in 1997, when she kindly responded to my advertisement asking former members of the WAAF to share their wartime memories with me. Little did I know then what a wealth of glorious memoirs, letters and commentary it would be my privilege to read over the next two years, and I am absolutely delighted that in this book they will be shared with a wider audience.

The pages that follow contain a vivid picture of wartime life in its infinite variety. Sylvia's letters home tell of the highs and lows of the local dances, the foibles of Sylvia's colleagues, and the endless search for an 'off-ration' cream bun during off-duty trips into local towns. Diary entries give a wonderful sense of both the variety and also sometimes the mundanity of Service life, detailing the films shown at camp cinemas, trips to sick-bay for cough-mixture, kit inspections, domestic evenings, and Sylvia's usually vain attempts to have an early night once in a while.

Letters from Roo, a Pilot Officer in the Royal Australian Air Force, describe so vividly the frustrations of being grounded for days on end in poor weather, the anti-climax of last minute stand-downs, and the intense and frenetic action of an operational sortie, all combined with a poignant reminder of the difficulties of romance in such a precarious situation. And Sylvia's wonderfully comic memories of the trials and tribulations of battling against intransigent Commanding Officers and dwindling supplies of pasture to graze her mare, 'Giddy Biddy', are a humorous antidote to the tragedy of wartime.

We are hugely in Sylvia's debt for breaking Service rules to write a diary, for keeping this wonderful selection of letters, and for weaving them together with an account of her wartime memories told with great eloquence and openness. For those readers who also served, *Tales of a Bomber Command WAAF* will evoke a wealth of shared reminiscences. For those, like me, who have experienced the Second World War only through the memories of others, this book adds another rich layer to our understanding of that momentous period of our history. It is indeed what Sylvia herself described as a 'perfectly ordinary story' of a WAAF at war—and as such it is a chronicle of some of the extraordinary people who did extraordinary things at an extraordinary time.

Dr Tessa Stone
Newnham College, Cambridge

INTRODUCTION

I want to explain how and why this book has been produced so long after World War II ended. For over fifty years I never gave a thought about the five years I spent as a clerk in the Womens' Auxiliary Air Force. It was not until there was much in newspapers, radio and TV that in the forthcoming Spring the country would be celebrating the 50th Anniversary of V.E. Day when, on 8th May, 1945 Victory in Europe was celebrated.

Then I thought back to my own teenage years, and how different life was in comparison with the freedom youngsters have today. I was a plump, plain bespectacled child, with my fine, mousey brown hair, tightly drawn back into two slim plaits. I was self-conscious about my appearance—during a year spent at Boarding School in Ambleside I was nicknamed "Whale". So, as a defence against teasing I unfortunately developed a very sharp tongue. I was totally honest, idealistic and conscientious—and always found it easier to make friends with animals rather than people. (I wonder why the word "prig" springs to mind?)

So it was that in 1995 I suddenly became nostalgic and wrote several little stories about my time in the WAAF, and I was delighted when the Imperial War Museum accepted them as worthy of retention, so I started to write connecting passages of my life and times.

In 1997 I opened a large box marked "Memorabilia" which we had carried around with us since clearing out our home at Saxilby ready for sale in about 1955. To my surprise and delight I discovered therein letters, which I had written to my Mother in 1941/42 and which she had cherished. Also other letters written to me from boy-friends. Reading these it brought home to me how greatly life and attitudes have changed since then. Thankfully a great deal has been published about those heroic men who so regularly faced danger and death in the skies but remarkably few WAAF have detailed their thoughts and feelings—particularly when they had a boyfriend in Bomber Command flying Lancaster bombers from 5 Group.

I did have some wonderful aircrew friends and I still treasure memories of the time we spent together. In those days "friends" did not automatically become "lovers". Our amusements did not include drug taking—apart from cigarettes. It was safe to walk alone anywhere, day or night, and to accept lifts with strangers in cars or lorries. Although there were numerous canteens for the Services, pay limited our spending in them so we did not have the problem of becoming overweight. There were no easily portable radios, television or mobile 'phones. "Surfing the Net" would have sounded like something to do with fishermen. I don't remember ever being bored.

The Imperial War Museum in London and the Second World War Experience Centre in Leeds have kindly accepted the originals of these letters for retention, and also have copies of everything else about my WAAF life that I have written, but I felt I would like to make it possible for others to see how those five tempestuous years changed me greatly. I had almost given up hope that a production of a book would be possible, however, in August, 2000 I met the charming Dawn Bowskill, who has a very kind heart and great skill with a computer. To my amazement she has kindly offered to prepare what I have written for publication. This is the result. I hope the "over 70's" may find it reminds them of times past, and that those under that age will have a glimpse into what it was like to live in the days long before they were born.

It may be wondered why I have included a photo of Frank, a letter from Cyril Whiteoak and a few from Bob Owens whilst at Coningsby; I did this to show that in wartime Service life friendships were often very brief, as one never knew when or what would cause that person to leave one's circle of friends either temporarily or permanently. You were friendly when within reach of each other but, generally speaking, did not expect to remain in contact indefinitely except for special deep friendships such as I was fortunate to have with Leslie, Roo and Ken during this period.

I should also mention that the punctuation etc. is not what one would find in any recently published book. I have not "modernised" it but have left it *exactly* as I originally wrote it. NOTHING has been changed except ONE adjective.

Sylvia Watts
July, 2002

1. *Enlisting at Harrogate*

Diary entries

Wed. 1 Jan 1941	W.A.A.F. call-up went <u>SHEFFIELD</u> then to <u>HARROGATE</u>[1] arr. 9 p.m. F.F.I. ("free from infection") inspection. Supper and bed in room 313.
Thur. 2 Jan 1941	Attestation. Waiting in queues. Given No. 426567. Kitted – skirt left for alteration. Wrote letters.
Fri. 3 Jan 1941	Saluting and Drill with Squad Cpl Barringer. Waited ¾ hr for Photog. outside in cold. "Ginger" mad as usual. Kit back from tailor.
Sat. 4 Jan 1941	Drill. Wore kit for 1st time. Lectures. "Morale" Inoculated against typhoid & tetanus.
Sun. 5 Jan 1941	Had breakfast then slept an hour. On to Church. About 50 C. of E. Unusual tunes for service. Good but slow sermon.

Grand Hotel, Harrogate (photo: Alice Gosling, late Autumn 2000)

[1] See Appendix I – WAAF Reception Centres

1

426567 A.C.W.2. PICKERING, J.S.

W.A.A.F. Depot, Grand Hotel, Harrogate

Sunday 5th January (1941)

My Darling,

I am pleased to find that I have plenty of time to write letters, as we have no work to do after tea, and we also have ½ Saturday and all Sunday free to do as we like.

It is really very difficult to remember what I have told you and what I have not, one thing I know you will be interested about, and that is leave. We have a week every 3 months, which I think is very good don't you?

We were asked in what part of the country we would <u>like</u> to serve – although the chances of being posted where you want to go is very slight – so I wonder if there is a chance of my going to Lincs, there are certainly plenty of aerodromes to choose from.

This morning there was a voluntary Church Parade for C. of E., Roman Catholic and other denominations, I counted nearly 50 of us that went to C. of E. We were led by a W.A.A.F. Sq Ldr and she had such a strange slow step that ½ of us could not keep in step. The Church we went to was St. Mary's, Harrogate. It was quite an old church, but no stained windows, and they sang the service in quite a different way to that we are accustomed to, and it was very difficult to follow; however, the sermon was quite good – but he spoke slower that Mr. Mann[1]. I am sure that even Anne[2] could have taken his sermon down in shorthand.

I don't know whether I told you that we have been kitted, and that I am sending home my things to-morrow. I am keeping the small suit-

---

[1] Mr. Mann was our Vicar at Saxilby. During his sermons I regret to admit that as a way of improving my skills I used to mentally take down his sermons in shorthand—I was doing a secretarial course in Lincoln.

[2] Anne was my cousin at boarding school in England as parents in Malta (R.N.) She spent her school holidays with us.

case as there is hardly room for anything in the kit bag, and one cannot keep shirts and collars nicely flat in the kit bag. I am very much appreciative of the hot water bottle this weather – as we too have quite deep snow here.

I have changed my trade to Clerk G.D. as when I had an interview I was told that M.S. Reader entailed about six months training (though I hear afterwards that it is only about six weeks). Even here they do not know what a M.S.R. does and as I did not want to buy a "pig in a poke" I said Clerk G.D. after all.

After only 4 days here we feel quite at home, more, in fact as if we had been here weeks instead of days. And it is very nice to see people coming in every day feeling strange, for at least we feel at ease. But early next week we shall either go to Pannal Ash or Ashville for a week's more advanced training. Here we never sleep more that 5 to a room but there we sleep in long, long dormitories – for we are supposed to be carefully "nursed" the first week, of course we have got the luxury of a first class hotel and 4 good hot meals every day and that does not make the discipline any less.

Yesterday morning a W.A.A.F F/Sgt gave us a short talk and then asked us to ask any questions which puzzled us, for she said that if we broke a rule it was no good saying that we "did not know" that rule – as ignorance was no excuse – for when we left here we were supposed to know everything about everything!

I am sure that I shall become fatter than I have ever been before because we do eat a lot, for instance today:

<u>Breakfast</u> Corn Flakes, Bacon and Baked Beans, Bread, Butter and marmalade, tea to drink.

<u>Dinner</u> Roast beef, Yorkshire pud., potatoes, sprouts. Apple pie.

<u>Tea</u> Bread, butter, lemon curd or jam, cold pressed beef, bacon and pickles. Cake.

Between meals we are continually buying things from N.A.A.F.I. One can buy cakes, buns, chocolate, tea, coffee, milk, ties, hairnets, collar studs, powder compacts, writing paper, Rinso, Andrews' Liver Salt, cigarettes, Aspro, stamps – in fact nearly everything you want.

Yesterday I wrote to them all at the Recruiting Centre[1] and I hope to write to Singleton[2] this evening. It's marvellous to have so much free time with absolutely nothing that needs doing.

Just now a small tabby cat has come along and settled itself on my knee and started to wash, and it has not made things very easy to write.

We have not had much drill as yet, but what we have had we have all enjoyed.

So far I think this training would do a world of good for Anne. When they tell you to be ready by 2.15 p.m. they usually mean 2.10. For instance several times we have been told to be ready to be taken down to breakfast at 7.20. And if you are not there by 7.15 they will already have gone. It seems strange to have to go before the appointed time to be ready.

(Another thing one has to get used to is always to take your knife, spoon and fork to meals. I have not seen a teaspoon since I have been here, and one never has a plate merely for bread butter and jam.)

Do take care of yourself, rest and don't worry, for I am very happy and shall see you again before three months is out.

If you have not already posted them don't forget to send my <u>GAS MASK</u> and <u>Ration Card</u>.

I will write again on about Wednesday, until then tons and tons of love from Bunty

---

[1] The Recruiting Centre was at Newport Barracks in Lincoln where I worked for the R.A.F. as a Clerk—my first job. This was when there was a rush of volunteers for the R.A.F. (particularly from the Lincolnshire Fens) and I had to call them for interview and send bus or railway warrants to them.

[2] Singleton was the R.A.F. Officer the Girl Guides found for an Examiner for a Guide Badge which involved knowledge of aircraft. I was their first candidate!

Diary entries

Mon. 6 Jan 1941	Drill. Inspection. "Standing Orders". P.T. Post Office shut, borrowed Pass. Went to "Virginia City" with Diana Flint.
Tues. 7 Jan 1941	Inspection. P. T. "Renewal of Kit". "Official Secrets". Recd. I. Cards from Ginger fury in Photo. Section. Went shopping with Diana.
Wed. 8 Jan 1941	Emergency posting to Ashville (College). Arr. Time for lunch. Our Squad drill with "Brylcreem"¹, Practised for pay day. First Aid Lecture. Sleep in "stalls" in Room 10, 20 of us in it.

No. 426567 W.A.A.F. Depot, Harrogate

Wednesday, 8th January, 1941

My Darling,

I am still enjoying my training immensely. Today we came to a slightly more advanced training centre about 2½ miles from the Grand.

Our kit was taken via lorry and we marched to this place in time for dinner. We were very sorry indeed to leave our Squad Cpl. Barringer – she was absolutely marvellous and we were all very, very fond of her.

Ashville College, as this place is called, was a boys' school, of course it is not so comfortable as the Grand for you cannot expect to always live in a first class hotel.

After an excellent lunch we had a first aid lecture, and then "Brylcreem" gave the ones who arrived today drill. There were about 26 of us and we were in fits of laughter. "Brylcreem" is supposed to be the original of the Brylcreem advertisements and he certainly looks like it too! He is a sergeant and you know what he looks like from the Brylcreem adverts! He makes the parade ground noises – and at first he asked why did not we keep step better – but we did not know when he said left and which was right. He was so sarcastic and mimicked us so amusingly that we were in _fits_ of laughter, which we had to try and keep down for fear he became cross.

---

¹ Brylcreem—a very effective masculine hairdressing cream

Thursday. Last night I found out that one cannot buy stamps from the N.A.A.F.I. and as I have lost my book of stamps I knew I could not post this letter, so did not finish it last night.

I find it frightfully difficult to write letters, for you know what a talker I am and there are always so many people to talk to. For the last hour I have had a very interesting talk with a girl who comes from Argentina. Her people own and breed, train and sell polo ponies. Once they sold one to the Maharajah of Bhopal for about £1,500 English money – it was an international player. She is an excellent rough rider, polo player and jockey. Her W.A.A.F. trade is to be private secretary to a senior officer. I asked her how she managed to get such a job and she informed me that she was a private secretary to the President of one of the largest firms in Argentina. – She is only just 24 and went to school at Sherborne and then back to Argentina. Isn't she a marvel?

This morning we all had "Fatigues" to do. Another girl and I had to go over all the building undoing the black-out and opening windows. Then we had a short break at N.A.A.F.I. and went to Sick Quarters and dusted a small 4 bed ward and then got down on our knees and scrubbed floors until 12 o'clock. We went back to the main building, cleaned our buttons again and got ready for dinner and we had a very good appetite.

In the afternoon we were, with all formality, paid. There were two officers there at the table, hence the extra polishing of buttons. Yesterday we were practising pay day with "Brylcreem", for this is what you have to do. When name is called stand smartly to attention and call out "Sir" and last 3 figures of your number. Advance to officer with Identity card in left hand. Salute with right hand. Transfer I. Card to r.h. pick up money with left. Left turn and march smartly away – luckily it is more simple than it sounds!

After pay a short route march and drill which was rather elementary as there were several newish people with us. A Gas lecture followed, it was rather boring as it was the last of four lectures and was consequently rather beyond us, but it will be alright when we have the earlier ones.

Then the Padre gave us a very nice talk on Morals, and compared the life of civilians with our Service life. I think everyone liked the lecture very much.

We were very ready for a good tea of finnan haddock. It is amazing what colossal appetites we have up here, for if we are ready for nothing else we are <u>always</u> ready in a queue for a meal! We seem to have 5 main jobs – eating, sleeping, cleaning buttons, drill and lectures.

We are now sleeping in a huge room which holds about 20, which is divided with wooden partitions between each bed – they look like rows of stalls in a stable, and it is all most amusing!

Reveille is supposed to be at 7 a.m. and we have to wake ourselves up, get washed and dressed, stack the bedrooms and be ready for breakfast by 7.50. After breakfast sweep out stalls and every alternate day we are given a Fatigue to do in the morning. The rest of the day is taken up by lectures on Gas, Discipline, Hygiene, First Aid, Standing Orders, A.R.P., Kit & Equipment and kindred subjects.

I shall probably be here for between a week or 14 days. And then, as I am a Clerk G.D. I shall be posted – oh, how I wonder where!

Last week I went with a chance acquaintance Diana Flint to the pictures. We saw "Virginia City", it was quite good, and we enjoyed the freedom. Diana is rather inclined to be a snob; she knows of Miss Dundass[1] quite well – she is supposed to be the richest and also the most miserly woman in the district.

I shall have to finish in a moment as it is almost 10.30 and "Lights Out". It is rumoured that the Post Box in this building is rarely cleared, and that it is safest to post them yourselves in Harrogate, so I fear this will probably not get posted until to-morrow night – so sorry darling.

My address is still the same as if I were at the Grand. Perhaps when I get settled down at a Station I shall write better and more regularly.

---

[1] Miss Dundass was my mother's Godmother.

Cheerio, darling, take care of yourself, love to all, but most for <u>you</u> my precious from

Bunty

Diary entries

Thurs. 9 Jan 1941	Black-out and Sick Bay fatigue. P.m. Pay-day 16/- Lecture "Kit & Equipment". "Gas Recognition". Drill and P.T.
Fri. 10 Jan 1941	"Ventilation". Talk by Padre. Stretcher Drill p.m. Drill and long route march. Dance Ripley Barracks. Went in lorries. Men ½ sozzled. Back 12.30
Sat. 11 Jan 1941	Drill. "Effects of Gas". Discipline & Fatigues". P.T. Moxon, Holman, Turk and I shopping, tea "Yorkshire Café". "Hired Wife". Visited Y.M.C.A. then Services' Club. 4 youths accompanied us back to Ashville. Yah!
Sun. 12 Jan 1941	Tired, stayed in bed until 11.30. read, wrote home and to Malta. Went to Pannal Ash (College) saw films "Majorca", "Horlicks", "Alf's Button Afloat". Freezing.

426567 A.C.W.2 PICKERING J.S.

Grand Hotel, Harrogate

Sunday, 12th January, 1941

My Darling,

I am still very happy, and I hope that you are too. I am sorry that my letters are posted so irregularly, but that can be remedied when I am posted.

Oh! how I wonder what part of the country it will be, I have an awful dread that they will post me on to Recruiting Duties, or else that I shall go to a Balloon Barrage Section. It will be a relief to know that it is either a Bomber or Fighter station.

Yesterday S/Ldr Singleton wrote to me and told me that it might be possible for me to wangle my way into a vacancy for a Clerk G. D. that his W.A.A.F. Officer had at Waddington. Unfortunately it is too late, as we have already been detailed to our stations, although we ourselves don't know where we are going to.

On Friday night a Sergeant came into our Recreation Room and said would any of us like to go to a Dance at Ripley Barracks. Four of my friends went, and we were called for by a lorry. There was a lorry load of about 15 from Pannal Ash our neighbouring College, 15 from Ashville and about 20 from the Grand and altogether we had 5 lorries to take us. They were really surprisingly comfortable, and ran nearly as smoothly as any car. I think I enjoyed the journeys more than anything else, for the only other good thing about was a good buffet with plenty of cakes price 1d each!

The men seemed to be the dregs of many regiments, and by midnight many of them had had more than was good for them to drink. But do not worry for me, darling. As long as I keep my good supply of common sense I do not think that any such experience can harm me in any way. In fact I think it is good for me, for I find that there is a very great deal of truth in the fact that "one half of the world does not know how the other half lives."

Yesterday the four of us went into Harrogate (2½ miles away) to do oddments of shopping such as hair nets, nail brush, powder puffs etc. After wandering round the shops we went to the Yorkshire Café and had a very nice tea. I had Fish Cakes and Chips (10d) and two meringues (3d. each). We had an excellent supply of cakes with lots of cream on them, and they were as good as almost any pre-war cakes.

After tea we went to see "Hired Wife", it was really most amusing and I quite enjoyed it. Then we thought we would go and see what the Y.M.C.A. had to offer. The refreshment room was packed with people eating plates of peas and potatoes and the air was so thick that we went out again quickly.

After a time we found our way to the United Services Canteen, which is a much smaller place. Here we were asked at once whether we liked tea or coffee, and soon after a girl came back bringing us each a salmon sandwich, a sweet H. & P. biscuit and a bun. No charge was made, we were merely asked to put something in the box at the door as we went out.

Coming back across one of the park like squares in Harrogate four youths asked if they might walk back with us, which they did. The other 3 girls are nice in every way except they are man-hunters. So I had no alternative but to make pleasant conversation. When we got back I said a charming good-bye, and left the other three to take a prolonged farewell! Talk about "pick-ups!!" But I know that you trust me, therefore I don't mind telling you all these funny happenings.

To-day I did not go to church, for I was very sleepy and did not like the service much last week. I stayed in bed and slept until 11.30 and am now writing letters. I have just written to Malta. This evening we are going to see a free Cinema Show at Pannal Ash, I think it is "Alf's Button Afloat" which is most amusing.

Lots of love, precious, from

Bunty

Sylvia – probably April/May 1941

Diary entries

Mon. 13 Jan 1941	Drill with "Brylcreem" First Aid P.T. Dinner. Route march. Personal Hygiene. How to put on Gas Masks. To bed early, Bath, wrote to M. Williams
Wed. 15 Jan 1941	Lectures. p.m. To Pannal Ash for pay.

Sylvia's Mother (probably about the same age here as I was during my WAAF days)

<u>My New Address will be</u>:-

426567 A.C.W.2. Pickering, J.S.

No. 14 O.T.U. R.A.F. Cottesmore

Wednesday, 15th January, 1941

Dearest,

What a thrill! At last I know where I am posted. It is an Operational Training Unit, whatever that may be! I have not got a map, but I don't think that I shall be uncomfortably far from home. All being well I shall have 48 hours leave within the next month, and then whoopee! you will see your little W.A.A.F.

I really feel too thrilled to write, so please excuse. To-morrow's programme begins like this:-

Check in blankets 6.30   Breakfast 7.15

Check in knife, fork and spoon.   Take down kit.

Transport leaves 8.00 hours.   Train dep. Harrogate 9.10

Change Nottingham, Melton Mowbray arrive Oakham 2.41 p.m.

Go to R.T.O.[1] to find out about ringing up for transport to take me to Cottesmore.

On Sunday I slept until nearly dinner time. Wrote letters and read P. G. Wodehouse. In the evening to a Cinema Show at Pannal Ash College ½ mile away. We saw a film of Majorca, the production of Horlicks and "Alf's Button Afloat". The last name is most amusing but unfortunately we did not have time to see it all through as we had to be in by ten o'clock.

This morning we had a lecture on the "Care and Construction of Gas Masks" followed by a route march in gas masks!

P.S.   The other ½ of letter posted by error in a great hurry.

Sorry. Love Bunty

---

[1] R.T.O.—Railway Transport Officer

Presumably this is the other half of previous letter:-

After the march we were vaccinated - we are feeling quite O.K. however.

Flight Officer Gray gave us a very interesting lecture on "Organisation and Administration in the R.A.F. as a whole and on R.A.F. Stations". She also told us about promotion, and to be an officer one needs outside sources for money, and that it isn't all jam at all!

I may have to end very abruptly as someone is going into Harrogate and says that she will take this letter. Otherwise it will not go until to-morrow.

I see on the list that there is a parcel for me, but cannot collect it until 6.30 I hope it isn't very....

Sketch map of Cottesmore area (not to scale)

2. *Posted RAF Cottesmore*

Diary entries

Thurs. 16 Jan 1941	Posted to 14 O.T.U.[1] Cottesmore. As far as Nottingham with 4 others. Transport met me Oakham. To camp film "Return of Dr. X" with "Tony".
Fri. 17 Jan 1941	Taken over to Armoury. F/Lt Johnson. W.O. Derbyshire. Sleep at Market Overton. Poor N.A.A.F.I. Filing.
Sat. 18 Jan 1941	Waited betwn 5-6.15 for bus in snow. Walked with Cpl. Hankey to C'more. Arr. Oakham 7 p.m. Pictures with "Harry". Cold. 4 cream buns. Bus stuck. Walked 1½ miles through drifts. Midnight.
Sun. 19 Jan 1941	5 A.G.s[2] spent night with us. Snowed up. Only lumpy porridge for breakfast. Rations of tinned food came for dinner. Got a rotten cold and throat temp. 99°.
Mon. 20 Jan 1941	Transport lorry (not bus) got through for us. To Sick Bay. Temp. 99°. More quinine. Excused duties 24 hrs. Wrote letters and read.
Tue. 21 Jan 1941	Temp. normal. E. D.[3] 24 hrs. Went back to work all the same. Masses of Amendments to 1644s etc. etc. Lac Thacker pushed file through finger. – He's jolly nice.
Wed. 22 Jan 1941	Back to duty – still to Sick Bay twice daily. Met "Biddy" – Thacker's girl. T. helped me with amendments. F/Sgt York showed me the A.M.L. Bombing Teacher.
Thur. 23, Jan 1941	Sick Bay for cough stuff – no good – cough worse! Not allowed to camp pictures – all back in Duty Lorry at 5.30 as since Sunday. Wrote Diary for last 10 days.

---

[1] O.T.U.—an Operational Training Unit where newly formed crews trained to work together in <u>twin</u> engined aircraft such as the Hampden or Wellington (Wimpy).

[2] A.G's—Air Gunners

[3] E. D. = Excused Duty

The Old Hall, Market Overton (photo by Leslie Watts 1998)

We were billeted in the lovely home of our WAAF Command-ing Officer, Lady Murray Smith at the Old Hall, Market Overton not far from R.A.F. Cottesmore. Other WAAF were billeted on the Camp in the houses near the Officers' Mess. As this was in the early days before Conscription sent reluctant females dashing to join the W.A.A.F in preference to entering munitions factories etc. our numbers were still quite small.

I believe I shared a bedroom with two or more cooks, for I think this was an early introduction to me of snobbish class distinction, which very much surprised me, as I was very na-ive and did not know such things happened. In the blacked-out darkness of our bedroom two girls were talking to each other, and one was telling the other about a super fellow she had just met and how much she would like to meet him again. She said they got on really well together until he asked her where she worked and she hated having to tell him it was in the cookhouse. She said "If only I didn't have to tell him I was a cook – if only I could have told him I was a clerk and worked in an office". I kept quiet, and the girls did not know that a clerk – me – had overheard the sad little story.

When I was younger my mother had tried to prepare me fully for life ahead! She arranged for me to have a Music Teacher come to give me lessons on our Piano at White Lodge. I was the reverse of "gifted" with my hands. Perhaps my Mother thought I was more likely to have success with feet rather than hands. Therefore, I had to submit to agonies of embarrassment at Ballroom Dancing classes held in an upstairs room in Silver Street, Lincoln. I knew no one there and they all seemed to be pretty, confident and capable. I was none of these. My feet were as clumsy as my hands. I used to be ramrod stiff with embarrassment and long for the time to arrive when I could scurry away and catch Hutson's hourly bus home from the Brayford.

Now you will realise why it took a lot of persuasion from the girls to get me to agree to accompany them to the dance in the Village Hall that bitterly cold January night in 1941! I lacked so much confidence that I even had a bet (two cream buns) with one of the girls, Marie Fuller, that no one would dance with me more than twice as I was such an inept dancer.

At the same time Leslie's hut mate, who was a very keen dancer, was trying to persuade Leslie to accompany him to the Dance, as he did not wish to go alone. Leslie was equally reluctant to leave the comparative warmth of the hut to trudge through snow on a bitterly cold January night just to keep his hut-mate company, but was eventually persuaded to do so. Leslie and I met at the Dance and danced together all evening. So I lost my bet! Here is what I told my mother about the Dance:

426567 A.C.W.2. PICKERING, J.S.
W.A.A.F. Mess R.A.F. Cottesmore
Monday, January 27th 1941

My Darling,

I am so sorry that I have not written to you for a week, it is amazing how quickly ones free time in the evening passes – buttons, shoes, make bed wash and iron a shirt mend stockings and that's another evening gone.

I am writing this at 8.30 in the morning, ready for work but hoping the F/Lt will not be back from breakfast yet. There is very little work to do as yet, and I often spend a very interesting time watching them at work in the armoury.

My cold is a lot better, and I am O.K.

Another girl called Gladys Rogers came up from Harrogate on Thursday. She is quite nice, and both being new we often pal together.

For the last week, ever since the snow, we have not been allowed out of camp. The Duty Lorry fetching us in the morning at 7.45 and taking us straight back to Mkt Overton at 6 o'clock after work. We are all fed up, or rather as we put it up here "browned off" or, alternatively, "cheesed off".

So on the Friday, on the spur of the moment Gladys and I decided to go to a Dance which was being held in the Village Hall.

I went with mixed feelings, wondering if it would be like my last one at Ripley Barracks.

When we got to the Hall I was very agreeably surprised to find a very good floor with curtains and a stage at one end.

I had betted one of the girls in our room 2 cream buns that I did not Dance with the same person more than twice. I hoped that I should find a nice partner, for it was exactly two years all except one day since Denis[1] took me to my first Dance, and somehow I felt that he was there too.

As a matter of fact I danced the whole evening continuously with a tall, fair, wavy haired R.A!!!!!![2] (Anne will be thrilled). He is <u>very</u> well educated (perhaps College?), lives at Oxford and is about 22 years old.

I know that you would like him, as he is "our" class of person, and it was such a surprise meeting such a "proper" person at that little village dance.

I am very much looking forward to next Friday as Gladys and I, and he and his friend are meeting there again. I never before realised how hot Service tunics are to Dance in – I felt as if I had had a Turkish bath, and wanted to keep putting my finger under my collar to loosen it.

(End of letter missing)

Denis on Bridget

---

[1]Denis was a super 6ft. 2ins. cousin who came up from Sandhurst to take me to my first formal Evening Dress Dance at the Assembly Rooms in Lincoln. I wore my first long dress of blue-green shot silk taffeta, which my mother had made for me. The photograph shows Denis on my mare Bridget. He was subsequently killed on the beach at Dunkirk.

[2] R.A. = Royal Artillery

Leslie was soon posted but we managed to meet and we spent many off duty hours together and I took him home with me to Saxilby when I had a 48 hr leave Pass. On one such occasion we missed our last bus from Grantham so we walked to the southern end of the town near the railway bridge over the road, and tried to get a lift. Lighting restrictions were so severe that even if there had been anyone willing to give us a lift it is doubtful if they would have been able to see us. So there was nothing for it but to try and find a bed for the night – or rather, <u>two</u> beds! Luckily there was a "B&B" sign up on a house nearby and so we were able to acquire bed<u>s</u> for the night. In the morning I can remember being very enthusiastically greeted by Leslie who came to my room. When I told my Mother what had happened she explained to me that we ought to have stayed in <u>different</u> houses – or at least on different floors if in the same house, or my reputation might be a little sullied!

In those days, particularly during the light summer evenings, it was very difficult to find anywhere private enough to have a kiss. I remember we once sought the seclusion of the Palm House in Lincoln's Arboretum, which was a most handsome building, now long since gone. I don't think we were very successful, as we were frequently interrupted by visitors there, whose only purpose was to admire the palm trees and the water lilies and the fish in the big ornamental ponds.

Not long before Leslie's Embarkation Leave was ending, I remember we were standing on the bridge over the railway line at Saxilby. We stood there together in silence. What had the Fates in store for us? Should we ever meet again? Suddenly, up the railway line, in the distance, a railway signal shone green in the darkness of the night. I said "It's an omen of good luck. Remember it. Have faith. You will return."

Diary entries

Mon. 3 Feb 1941	Gladys and I and 2 Bobs to C[1]. films. "Ghost Breakers". Marvellous film.
Wed. 5 Feb 1941	To S/Ldr Bright with ankle – he is fine.
Thurs. 6 Feb 1941	To Camp Pictures with Gladys and 2 Bobs. "Enemy Agent" "Confidential Lady" All walked back across 'drome – ankle worse next day.
Fri. 7 Feb 1941	Sq/Ldr Weir came in and suddenly barked "take a letter". Lazy blighter. Gladys went for a long walk with Bob and got lost – back 11.30 p.m. 1st German Class in H.Q.
Sat. 8 Feb 1941	Fl/Lt J. away until 12.30 F/S Gale and W/O off duty. Finished typing "Banquet" and Range Orders. Gladys and Bob on 48 hr pass. Ironed shirts and to bed early.
Sun. 9 Feb 1941	F/O Frome with ankle – nice. Excused P.T. Arranged visit to Leadenham – Cancelled owing to Hampden[2] crash for 3rd time. Mild and drizzly.

There were no more diary entries in 1941.

I found my work for the Station Armament Officer very interesting, but also very technical. At first there was not much work for me to do in the office so I used to spend every opportunity in the Armoury itself, learning how to identify different ammunition and guns. The Armourers used to quiz me to test, for example, whether I could tell the difference between Armour Piercing and Tracer ammunition. Being such a "sprog" (new) the armourers naturally wanted to catch me out by sending me to the Stores for some non-existent item of equipment. At first I was sent to the Equipment Section to ask for a "A Long Stand". Luckily I knew that all I should get was "A Long Wait". Eventually I was caught out – and victory was theirs! I was sent out for "A BOX OF BOMB

---

[1] C. = Camp

[2] Many crashes due to lack of experience of the pilots.

SIGHT BUBBLES". I was very reluctant to go, as I did not think there were such things – however, F/Sgt "Stormy" Gale, who gave me the order, looked as if he might indeed live up to his nickname, so I duly went on my mission. I thought "Bomb Sight Bubbles" just MIGHT be little glass beads! Imagine the hoots of joyful laughter when I returned – they had caught me out at last!

Early in 1941 it was thought that the enemy might try to land at any time, by air or sea. Apparently most airmen on the Camp were not keen on trying to improve their ability with rifle or revolver. So the Armament Officer, my boss, was quite happy to take me down to the 25 yard Range on the edge of the Camp, where I became quite proficient with the .38 Smith & Wesson revolver, but less successful with the heavier .45.

I enjoyed firing the S.M.L.E.[1] .303 Rifle with the "V" sights from the prone position, as otherwise it was too heavy for me. I also tried my hand with the Twin Vickers G.O.[2] guns as used in the Hampden aircraft in those days, but they and the "Tommy" Guns were, I felt, more in control than I could have wished!

I still treasure a silver teaspoon which displays two crossed rifles, the initials WDRC and engraved with the name *T. Pickering* and the date 1902; this was won by my father some-where in Lincolnshire – I wish I knew where.[3] So I knew how pleased he would be if I became a good shot too.

The plan was that I was to encourage other WAAF to become proficient enough to form a team – and then the WAAF would challenge the R.A.F. to a competition. The Station Ar-

---

[1] Short Magazine Lee Enfield

[2] Gas Operated

[3] Mrs. Joyce Pickering suggests this might have been Wragby District Rifle Club.

mament Officer hoped that the fear of being beaten by a team of WAAF might stir the men into more effort down on the range! Unfortunately, just when we had got quite a good WAAF team trained, and were ready to challenge the men, the Air Ministry decreed that in future no airwomen would be allowed to use Service arms, ammunition or Ranges. So that was an end to that.

Two of the Armourers were named Bob. One had black hair and the other ginger. My WAAF friend Gladys Rogers and I often used to go to the Camp Cinema with them. I went with "Black Bob" and Gladys partnered "Ginger Bob".

I had my first "proper" kiss with "Black Bob" and it would not surprise me if he was as inexperienced at this pleasant occupation as I was.

I remember thinking "this first kiss is supposed to be something special – I must remember all about it". In reality I don't think it was all that memorable for either of us. It probably took place somewhere between the Camp Cinema or the N.A.A.F.I. and the top of the hill where our transport used to wait to take us back to the little village of Market Overton (or Market Chuff-Chuff as we used to call it for some inexplicable reason).

Gladys Rogers

One dark, bitterly cold night that winter "Black Bob" and I were running through the Camp so that I could catch the transport, which took the WAAF back to Market Chuff-Chuff. It was imperative for me to catch it or I should have been stranded. I don't know why we were so late. Perhaps we had dallied on our way back from the camp cinema and had found a private pool of darkness in which to gain further practice in this newly-found sport of kissing.

Perhaps my kisses were better than I had realised, for as we ran panting up the hill to the waiting lorry "Black Bob" said, in between gulping for breath, "Will you marry me?"

I remember thinking, with shocked horror, that this was not the way in which one's first proposal of marriage should be received – a more unromantic situation could hardly be imagined – nevertheless, I determined to remember when and where this happened so that, when an old lady (in lavender and lace?) I might try to relive the memory of that first real kiss and proposal of marriage.

426567
ACW/2 Pickering, J.S.
W.A.A.F. Mess,
R.A.F. Station, Cottesmore

Thursday, 20th February, 1941

My Darling,

How marvellous it was to see you again last week, although it was for only a short time.

The train arrived outside Grantham just as the sirens went, and we waited outside the Station for ten minutes or so.

I managed to find a Canteen just outside the station and had a cup of tea and a lemon curd tart. I did not stay for long as I did not want to risk not being able to find the Bus place and missing it. I arrived back at Market Overton at 9.45, so it was good going wasn't it? I need hardly say that the bed did not seem as comfortable as the one I had the night before!

Everyone very much enjoyed the Swiss roll, it was <u>beautifully</u> light and had not suffered much from the journey – it looked quite O.K. when pressed back into shape!

The Armoury thought that I looked very much better for my 48, and I certainly felt it too.

On Tuesday the four of us (Gladys, 2 Bobs and I) went to an E.N.S.A. Concert which was held in the Airmens' Mess. It was <u>very</u> good, better than either of the two previous concerts we have had. One fellow did some exceedingly clever lightning sketches with coloured chalks of the British Grenadiers when the pianist played that tune, of an old

Scotsman's head and shoulders for "Bonnie Scotland". He also did a remarkably good likeness of a fellow whom he invited out of the audience. He really was a wizard with those chalks and it seemed so effortless to him – just a few quick lines and – hey presto!

Yesterday I went to German again, and was bored stiff. I ought not to go to this elementary German but to the advanced. The advanced is on Mondays and Thursdays, both Camp picture nights, so that puts an end to that.[1]

Afterward the four of us went back to the Armoury for a cup of tea and some buns. Bob I was Duty Armourer, and could not leave the Armoury so we had to go there, you see! We caught a bus back to Market Overton, for which I was very thankful, as you know how much I like walking!

To-night we 4 are going to the Camp pictures – it is ten days since I have seen a film which is an amazingly long time on this Station. One just goes to them – it does not matter what is on, you just take them as they come.

I was told that Emerton was acting in the one last Monday, what a pity I missed him.[2]

Lots of love and a terrific bear hug

My darling,

From Bunty

---

[1] Pre-war a German Westphalian student had lived with us to teach me German.

[2] He was an R.A.F. Officer at the Lincoln R.A.F. Recruiting Centre where I had worked.

3. *Bridget – my nightmare*

It is probably unfair of me to describe Bridget as my nightmare for she was only just a little bright bay mare which my father bought for me when I grew too big to ride my small pony Peter. I believe my Mother must have gone with my Father to see some prospective purchases for I am told that when my Mother was told that Biddy had been bought for me my Mother remarked "Surely you haven't bought that hot headed mare for her?" He had. Bridget duly arrived and a stable was built for her in the back garden of our semi-detached house in Saxilby and grazing rented for her at, I believe, five shillings per week (25p).

Pete gives me a kiss on the back lawn at home, whilst cousin Anne and Punch look on. Bridget looks the other way.

Stamped on Bridget's two front feet were letters and numbers which indicated that she had recently seen service in the Army. I had a cousin, Denis, at Sandhurst at the time and he was able to find out that from the numbers Bridget had been in the 2nd Battalion Royal Ulster Fusiliers and he discovered that they had recently been sent out to India, hence Bridget was "de-mobbed" and sold on. All my teenage friends longed to have a ride on Bridget as she was bigger and faster than their ponies but she was soon nicknamed "Giddy Biddy" as she always wished to race everything and her brakes were often almost non-existent. She bolted with everyone at least once, including me, and would only let herself be pulled up when she was well in front and had had a good gallop.

When I joined the WAAF Bridget had to come with me as there was nowhere she could be left at Saxilby, I did not want to part with her, and she wasn't a safe enough ride to lend to any of my friends.

Much grassland was ploughed up in wartime, which made it extremely hard to find any suitable grazing to rent. Consequently I used to have the most awful nightmare – the same one over and over again – I was leading Bridget along a straight road, alongside which were lush grass paddocks lined with big thick hedges and shady trees. Strong five-barred gates with huge padlocks on them protected all the fields. I had to keep on up this road leading Bridget with no chance of turning her into any of these grassy havens to rest and graze. My nightmare.

As a child I had always been fascinated with anything to do with flying, so it is not surprising that I joined the WAAF as soon as I was able to do so. Once posted to R.A.F. Cottesmore in the old county of Rutland I was lucky enough to meet Mr. Fountain who farmed in the middle of Cottesmore village and very kindly let me put Bridget in a field close to his farm. I kept my saddle and bridle in one of his barns so was able to bike to the village and have a ride on my day off. All trace of house and buildings have now been removed – it is merely a potential building site adjacent to the Church.

We WAAF soon left Market Overton and were then billeted at the handsome Exton Hall a couple of miles away. At least I imagine it was handsome but don't remember seeing the outside of it in daylight as we were transported into R.A.F. Cottesmore Camp for breakfast when it was still dark and it was just as dark when we were taken back at night – always to the back door.

Exton Hall – front of house (photo by Leslie Watts 1999)

A group of us had beds placed around a huge room, which may well have been a ballroom in happier days, and I seem to remember tall windows with close fitting wooden shutters on them.

My bed was sited immediately behind the door which led into the room so that if anyone opened the door too far it banged against my bed. An example of how soundly I slept in those days is that, on one occasion, a WAAF in one of the beds was taken ill during the night. She was eventually taken from the room on a stretcher. In the morning I asked why this girl's bed was empty. No one would believe me when I said I had slept through all the commotion of the previous night and was unaware that, with some difficulty, she had been carried out of the room on a stretcher close to my bed.

Grounds of Exton Hall (photo by Leslie Watts 1999)

Our stay at Exton Hall did not last long for we heard rumours that Australians were coming there instead of us. We were to be moved further away to the east of the Great North Road to Clipsham Hall where there were just a few houses and a quaint little pub called "The Olive Branch" – which we soon nick-named "The Twig".

It was delightfully rural and peaceful and I shared a large bedroom on the first floor. This overlooked the splendid park and carved emblem of the Davenport Handley's over the front door, and there was a large gravelled area and lawns edged by huge old trees. In the summer months of the year we were woken by pheasants calling to each other and on looking out of the window they could be seen strutting about outside on the gravel. There was a huge grassy park beyond studded with mature trees and some gorgeous old indoor stables with huge loose boxes in them surmounted by iron railings above their wooden divisions. The sort of place you might find today, which had been restored by the National Trust in one of their properties – now being used as a Shop or Tea Room. I think you can guess what I was thinking!

Clipsham Hall (photo by Leslie Watts 1996)

One day I managed to meet the owner of Clipsham Hall, Mr. Davenport Handley, and had a most interesting chat with this distinguished gentleman about his famous Clipsham Quarries, stone from which was used in the construction of the Houses of Parliament and other well known London landmarks. Mr. Davenport Handley was quite agreeable for Bridget to graze in his Park and for me to use his stables for her. I was thrilled – I had never before seen such sumptuous stables, let alone had the use of them. So I wrote off to my WAAF C.O. requesting what I thought would be a mere formality, namely, that I could go ahead with what Mr. Davenport Handley was happy for me to do. I was surprised to receive the following copy of a letter, which the C.O. of R.A.F. Cottesmore had sent to the WAAF C.O:

Ref: Cot/451/27/P.1   Date: 2nd May, 1941

Application – 426567 ACW.2 Pickering, S.Clk.GD

The application of the above-named airwoman to keep a horse at Clipsham Hall is not approved.

2.   It is noted that she has already approached Mr. Davenport Handley on the subject.

3.   The practice of individual airwomen approaching the owners of requisitioned property for favours is to cease. In the interests of the Service, it is desirable to remain on good terms with the owners of requisitioned property, and it will be difficult to maintain such good terms if they are worried by airwomen continually for small favours.

4.   All negotiations with the Owners should come through the Station Administrative Officer.

(signed)

Group Captain, Commanding

R.A.F. Station, Cottesmore

Needless to say I was very disappointed as Bridget was five or six miles away at Cottesmore whilst I was at Clipsham. Mr Fountain became very short of grass so I took a chance and moved Biddy to the palatial stables and the vastness of Clipsham Park. I was careful to wipe out her hoof prints in the gravel round the house when I had had occasion to ride her up to the N.A.A.F.I. van when it made its call there. Bridget ungratefully repaid me by preferring the wide open spaces of the Park to being ridden and usually refused to be caught unless I had managed to persuade a number of people to help me corner her.

I remember on one hot summer day she had been particularly cussed. When she was finally caught, saddled and bridled I rode back into the Park, threw down the reins and threatened to give her a beating for taking us an hour to catch her! Bridget knew I would not hit her but it gave her freedom to have a good gallop. Normally I could not have the luxury of a flat out gallop on Biddy as there was never enough space to pull her up in once she got going. However, I eyed the wide open grassy expanse of the Park and thought I had at last got the ideal place to let her go as fast as she wished.

I suppose we were approaching 30 m.p.h. when I suddenly realised that I was flying through the air – alone! Then I hit the ground, rolling over and over several times before I was able to stagger to my feet, feeling very dazed. I dashed back to Bridget and grabbed the reins in case she decided to gallop off solo. I know that we stood close together in the Park for a considerable time, both of us quaking from the force and unexpectedness of our fall. Thankfully Biddy was not injured. I think the top of a rabbit or mole run had probably given way beneath her pounding hooves, which caused our crash.

The Armourers from the Station Armoury where I worked as a Clerk often used to do Range Duty at Grimsthorpe Castle Bombing Range and they invited me to ride over to visit them on a day off. It was quite a long hack for me from Clipsham on strange country roads and with no signposts to guide me. Eventually I agreed to ride over to see them.

Grimsthorpe Park is huge, after all, it must be if it was big enough to contain a Practice Bombing Range. I remember riding in the park and wondering whether or not it was safe to do so. I cannot remember whether or not I did see a red flag flying or whether I saw a red flag flying and then looked for signs of an aircraft which might be about to make a bombing run. I do remember seeing just one aircraft high up in the blue sky at right angles to our track and flying straight and level. I think it was a Hampden but it was so high up that I couldn't imagine that its presence could possibly concern us. I was wrong.

Shortly afterwards there was a heavy thud on the ground quite close to us and white smoke belched out of a fallen object – a practice bomb! Bridget took fright and shot off at full gallop and happily took me with her.

We never did find our friendly Armourers that day, as we felt we did not know when the next bomb might drop or, more importantly, where. Anyway Bridget said her nerves were shattered and she wanted to leave the range as fast as possible – so we did just that.

What a headline we could have made in the newspapers – "WAAF and horse killed on bombing range by the Royal Air Force"!

426567 ACW/1 Pickering, S.

Station Armoury, R.A.F. Cottesmore, Rutland.

Wednesday, 10th December, 1941

Dearest One,

At last I have a few minutes in which I can write to you, although I don't know how long it will be before I am rudely interrupted. I simply must tell you what fun I had yesterday out hunting.

The Meet was not at Greetham itself as I had thought, but at Greetham Inn Farm on the Gt. North Road about 3 miles away. I went to the Mess for breakfast in my riding kit, and managed to persuade the Mess Staff to cut me some sandwiches with my Marmite, and I then walked to Cottesmore to see about Bridget who they (the Fountains) had promised to fetch and feed for me.

As I passed the Park where she lives I saw a boy with a bowl of oats and Bridget walking round and round in circles. Bridget trying to get the oats and then dashing off, and the boy trying to catch her! The wall round the Park was about shoulder high, and the high wooden gate locked but I managed to scramble over leaving my bridle and beautifully blancoed[1] girth on the pathway. Luckily she allowed me to catch her and we took her to the stable.

They got her a lovely breakfast of oats and chaff and hay. She was a muddy mess, but I managed to get her quite presentable and plaited her mane and tail. At least I tried to plait except at the top which I had to try and sew tidy! Her tail was like one of those modern pictures – a real work of art but not quite definite what shape or form it was supposed to take!

Owing to a very sharp frost the Meet was postponed until 12 o'clock but I did not know that until I got there. Only a few people were out, and I will describe them as best I can for I shall probably meet them again if I get some more hunting.

The Master is a Mr. Illsley Green (or something like that), and he and his wife are terrifically keen. Yesterday there was an oldish huntsman hunting with Mrs. I.G. helping him. She is rather nice, probably in her forties, uses make up out hunting ('tho neatly) and has brightly varnished nails underneath her string gloves. She is also inclined to be a trifle plump, 'tho I cannot judge her fairly as I have only seen her on her horse. I am told that she is a very good horsewoman and goes like blazes.

---

[1] Blancoed—whitened with Blanco, normally used to whiten tennis shoes

There was another woman in her early thirties or late twenties riding on a very big black horse. She was small and the horse seemed very hefty for her, especially as she was riding side saddle. She was quite nice too.

Another man was called 'Eddy' he was a largish chap, extremely round shouldered with a walrus moustache and a bowler hat which he always kept tilted forward at such an angle that you could scarcely see his eyes at all. He was the type that when they gallop his arms flopped up and down like a scrawny old hen.

There was a girl in her late twenties riding a black pony (about 14.2 hands) trace clipped and I imagined that she was one of the Old Brigade for she seemed to know her way about very well, and was well in with Mrs. I.G.

The horse I liked best was ridden by a Mr. Riddall (or something) from Cottesmore, it was a chestnut with very nice action and a good jumper. He has another chestnut and a grey up and clipped so must be a regular follower. When we were coming away and commenting on the poor scent he seemed to waggle his head and twitch his nose – I thought he was alluding to the scent but luckily did not remark on it. He did it so many times on the way home that I have come to the conclusion that he could not help it. He was in the Air Force during the last war.

There was one other person who puzzled me extremely because I could not make out whether she was a man or woman. This person was riding an unclipped black pony (14.2) which I heard tell was a wonderful jumper. Had short cropped hair, a bowler hat jammed on tightly, and a mannish voice – the only way I got a solution was by noticing that she was using a small amount of lipstick, otherwise I should never have known.

Last but not least (not by any means least), there was a girl in a most appalling rig-out – sans boots, sans hat, sans hunting crop, riding a well bred but moth eaten animal. Its mane was a series of hairy lumps supposed to be plaits, (and those of the girl weren't much better), and its tail looked as if someone had been tying knots in it and matting it together. Admittedly it was fat, but lumps of mud were sticking all over its tum and elsewhere – oh what a pair! (But we showed 'em!)

No doubt you will have gathered that it was a small but select crowd which partook of hunting that day. We went to some coverts on the other side of the North Road, but did not do more than gallop once or twice up and down the wood. In spite of doing so little Bridget was puffing and blowing like an over fed sea lion doing the rumba, so I was determined not to have her out for long. Accordingly, when we gave those woods up as a bad job and came back to Cottesmore to have a drink at Mr. R's I thought I would finish, but it was only 2.15 and was persuaded to stay longer. We then went down into Ashwell Vale which is towards Oakham and drew there.

I was very much wondering what would happen if we came to some jumps as I have not jumped her out hunting for two years, and I had not got a crop to persuade her with, and I did not want to let the Burton country down when I went with the cream of the hunting counties. Hounds found and started running; the best way seemed to be over a post and rails which Mr. R. cleared well, so I put on plenty of speed and determined to follow.

Much to my relief we cleared it and went racing over the grass and two more lots of posts and rails, one of which was quite a decent size. As I looked round I saw two of the others refuse and my heart was full of glee, and I determined that where that chestnut could go we could go too – although we probably couldn't really. We checked then, and one of them, I forget which, came up and congratulated me on Bridget's jumping, and said what beautiful style she had! Yahoo! We'll larn 'em teach 'em, teach 'em larn 'em!!!!

Bridget was now pulling like blazes, almost bolting in fact, anyone would have thought that she was up and fed on oats and exercised every day to see how keen she was, and she did not seem to blow at all. Down an old canal bank and up the other side, with her trying to gallop down it sideways, along an ironstone quarry railway track at break neck speed. It was wizard. It wasn't really a run, for the scent was so poor, but a wonderful gallop over and round about a dozen fields.

We saw the fox come out of the gorse in the field with hounds at the other side of the field, and if scent had only been better he would certainly have been a deader!

I was back at Cottesmore by 4.15 and everyone came out to welcome us – a bucket of warm water for her Ladyship, a great trough full of oats and chaff and hay with other tasty additions to tempt her appetite brought without my even asking for them. They told me not to wait to turn her out myself, as they would do it for me later when she had fed and was cool, and that any time I wanted to go hunting they would fetch her up early and feed her for me. Wasn't that sweet of them?

I then walked back to Exton and had a hot bath, ate my huge pile of sandwiches and went to sleep. Gee, was I stiff next day or was I. I am still walking bow-legged! With much wangling and wheedling the F/Lt. has consented to let me go hunting again to-morrow if it is a fine day and Bridget is O.K. for the Meet is only five miles away at South Witham.

This evening I am having my hair washed and set in Oakham to be followed by a Dance to show it off! My very great pal Mary Wood is coming too, Vic is going down to Cottesmore first to ask them if they will be kind enough to fetch Biddy up for me to-morrow morning, and then he is probably joining us at the Dance. (I wonder if the Army Officers will be there).

I have just written an Airgraph to Les. and hope that it will reach him. What fun we used to have together, I am enclosing his Airgraph, and hope that you will be able to read it – you will need a magnifying glass.

By the way, did any of your stamp deals come off? When shall I have my '48' for this month? Shall I have my leave in this quarter of Dec. Jan. Feb or have 14 days in the following quarter?

Take care of yourself sweetest,

LOVE,

Bunty

P.S.   *I am remembering to take the Radiostoleum[1].*

P.P.S.   *Don't forget love to Daddy too.*

Frank

Frank was one of a group of Army Officers met in Oakham. I remember having dinner with him in a lovely old stone hotel in a secluded square in Oakham. Subsequently Frank came over to meet me at the attractive village pub whilst I was bil-

---

[1] Radiostoleum—cod liver oil capsules

leted at Exton Hall. When Frank asked me what I would like to drink I naturally wanted to appear sophisticated and a "woman of the world" so decided that the choice of a sherry would not create the impression I wished to make. My thoughts went back to the April of 1939 when, as a sixteen year old, my Mother and I went to Malta during the Easter holidays so that my cousin Anne could spend her holiday with her parents as Uncle was a Naval Captain stationed there. I quickly remembered that on social occasions at that time hearing people asking for "a gin and bitter" so, thought I, that is the "in" thing to do. So I did just that. I would have been perfectly happy with "a gin and lime", for example, but alas, the addition of Angostura Bitters made it look a pretty pink but was AWFUL! It was very hard to try and look as if I was enjoying it.

When staying on leave in Reading I did once visit Frank at his parent's home in Camberley where they lived quietly in retirement.

All the Officers and Senior NCOs, as was customary, served Christmas Dinner, to us. We each had a copy of the traditional Christmas Menu (see following pages), which we passed round the table for autographs from our particular friends. Gladys Rogers, my particular friend, who arrived at Cottesmore a week or two after I did, and Doris MacKenzie, a Scot with a lovely accent head the list of names on my copy! Mabel Utting was older and more serious than most of us and became our Librarian. Marie Fuller was the girl with whom I had the bet of two cream buns about dancing more than twice with the same partner when I first met Leslie in January.

Overleaf on the Menu is Roo's "Happy Memories Cherie" – I had met him only very recently – much more will be heard of him later.

Doris Mackenzie

On this Christmas Day we had wonderful amounts of super food which was strictly rationed for the other 364 days of the year. It was wonderful to feel "full". I know I had at least two lots of everything and would have loved to lie on my bed to sleep off the effects but our Billets were several miles away from the Mess Hall on the Main Camp. Mary Wood had arranged to meet her friend Les Hollins, the Link Trainer Instructor in the Link Room; a Link Trainer was a trademark for a flight simulator device used to train aircrew. There were

41

probably only two chairs in the room and that is why I could not find anywhere to sit to recover from my overeating. I think this is why I ended up trying to go to sleep on the parquet floor as there was nowhere else to sit. I was not very comfortable.

Until it was recently pointed out to me I had not realised how many of my letters home mentioned food and how much it cost. This seemed perfectly natural to me for food was so strictly rationed that we always had a very good appetite for anything "off ration" – provided we could afford it on our meagre pay. I believe that these days at least one in three people are overweight. There was no fear of that happening to us – although we were much better off than the civilians as we had the N.A.A.F.I. and various canteens.

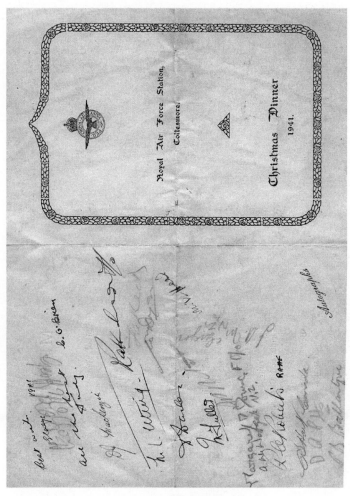

Christmas Menu 1942.

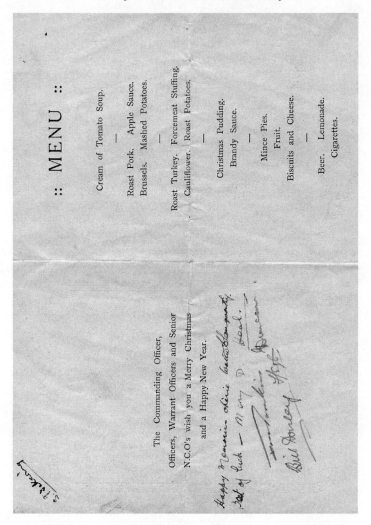

Christmas Menu 1942.

4. *The pyjamas and the tin hat*

I think it was probably through necessity rather than choice that my Mother always used to head for the Remnant Counter at the January Sales, to see what bargains she could find in the way of odd lengths of material which she could make up into clothes, cushion covers or things of that kind. I don't think that in my childhood I observed her sufficiently closely so that I could say whether or not this fetish from which she suffered was connected with the onset of the war and clothes rationing or not.

I do remember that in the far corner of the dining room next to the huge light oak sideboard with its deep cupboards and mirrored overmantel (a legacy from my Father's farming days when he lived in large old farmhouses which could easily accommodate such things) stood a cheap looking stained softwood cupboard with a shelf in it. This was known as my Mother's "Glory Hole" into which were crammed all her sewing bits and pieces – remnants, clothes which needed either altering or completing. The door to this cupboard opened easily enough – its contents tended to cascade on to the carpet in a gloriously coloured jumble. When the time came to close the door, however, that was a different matter for the contents of the cupboard suddenly seemed imbued with a life of their own and all desired their freedom. They fought vigorously before they were imprisoned once more.

I can only think that it was from the "Glory Hole" that my Mother found the material to make me the pyjamas referred to in the above title. Strangely these are the only pyjamas or night-gowns that I have worn that I could describe. They are printed so indelibly on my memory that I feel I could walk into the bathroom, reach into the warmth of the airing cup-board and bring them out and show them to you. No, they were nothing very daring or unusual – they weren't fifty years ago. They were of a lightweight material in a cheerful orangey-yellow colour with thin pencilled lines down the ma-terial in a dark chocolate hue. They were short sleeved as I believe my Mother did not have enough material in the rem-nant to make them more than elbow length. The collar and cuffs were in a plain dark chocolate colour as were the turn-ups on the rather bell-bottomed trousers. The finishing touches were the chocolate material covered buttons down the pyjama jacket front. They did not look suitable pyjamas for a man to wear in 1941.

One 48 hour Leave Pass was usually granted to all WAAF personnel every month. It was possible to cadge a lift to the Ram Jam Inn on the Great North Road or A1 as it is usually known these days. Despite the shortage of petrol there was quite a lot of traffic which stopped there for liquid or other refreshment and it was an excellent place to find a driver kind enough to give a WAAF in uniform a lift.

At that time we did not know whether the Germans would use gas in any raids on this country and it was mandatory to take with us, whenever we went out of doors, our steel helmet and gas mask. The former fitted quite snugly on top of the case of the latter.

As I was planning to hitch-hike to relations in the county of Lincolnshire, which bordered Rutland, I intended to travel as light as possible – as far as I was concerned the tin hat and gas mask was load enough for me. The afore described pyjamas were rolled up tightly and pushed inside my tin hat for the journey. They had travelled this way before on previous 48 hour passes so I knew I should not lose them provided I periodically remembered to check that one silky pyjama leg had not escaped the confines of the tin hat and was trailing gaudily behind me. After all if one leg escaped, no doubt, the other might do so also.

F/Lt Johnson was a super person to work for. Strictly speaking Leave did not begin until work had finished for the day but I knew he was likely to be generous and would give me a chit to show at the Guard Room so that I could begin my leave early. So, there I was, in the office we shared together when the telephone rang and my boss answered it and put the 'phone down again saying that the C.O. wanted to see him immediately. He hadn't got his tin hat and gas mask with him and he couldn't go to see the C.O. without one, so "You don't mind if I borrow yours do you?" What could I say? I was too shy to say "You can, but do be careful my very feminine gaudy pyjamas don't fall out while you are in with the C.O.". So I kept quiet and prayed hard. It seemed ages before he returned, thanked me and hung up the gas mask again on the peg near my chair. All was well. My prayers had been answered. As the hymn had it – "All was safely gathered in."

5. *Is it wise to tell the truth?*

If I had been more economical with the truth my time in the WAAF might have been very different. It seems likely that I could have had much more pay, better food, a smart uniform – with a batwoman to clean my buttons for me – and much more comfortable and warmer living accommodation. In other words, if I had played my cards right, I might have become a WAAF Officer. This is what happened.

Right from early childhood I have always felt impelled to tell the truth. I wish I knew why. I remember it being explained to me that if I was asked, for example, "Do you think this hat/dress suits me?" I should be careful that my reply did not hurt or offend my questioner – even if this necessitated the truth being "bent" a little. I remember staunchly defending my stand by saying that I would rather that people replied honestly to my questioning than by saying what they thought I wanted to hear to my face and saying something different behind my back.

When I worked for F/Lt Johnson the correspondence for him used to be delivered from Station Headquarters already filed. It was signed for and put on his desk for action. However, because the Armoury correspondence was so technical the unfortunate Assistant Adjutant at S.H.Q.[1] frequently put things in the wrong file. As a result it was eventually agreed that we should be the only Section on the Station to be in

---

[1] S.H.Q. = Station Headquarters

charge of all its own files. They were kept in our office and the correspondence then came over from S.H.Q. loose, in a large envelope, and I dealt with the filing myself, having everything listed and filed ready in F/Lt Johnson's IN tray ready for his arrival in the morning.

This new arrangement suited me fine. Until that happened I had had to go on Parade after coming in to the Camp for breakfast and be inspected before we were all dismissed to go about the camp to our different duties.

F/Lt Johnson wrote me a chit to permanently excuse my going on Parade saying that he needed me to go early to his Office in order to prepare the mail for his attention. This was super, it gave me plenty of time to do my hair and "put on my face" in the peace and quiet of the office, instead of having to be ready for a detested Parade half an hour or so earlier.

All went along happily until I was told one day that the WAAF C.O. wished to see me that morning. Naturally enough such a summons was worrying. What had I done that she might have found out about? Happily I found that my conscience was clear (this was before the days when I kept my mare at Clipsham Hall despite having had a letter from the C.O. forbidding me to do so).

To my surprise I was asked whether I had ever thought of applying for a Commission in the WAAF. It was suggested that I might like to apply to be Commissioned and become an Assistant Adjutant. What were my feelings on the subject?

Now I had always been led to believe that the R.A.F. Station Adjutant had an Assistant Adjutant to do his bidding and that this person usually led a "dog's life". So my reply was not exactly enthusiastic. A Commission would obviously give numerous material advantages, however, I was very happy in the Armoury with my super boss and plenty of congenial Armourers for company. So I spoke the truth as I saw it. I said that my parents would be very pleased if I gained a Commission and I would like to make them happy. However, if I became a WAAF Officer I should be limited in my choice of friends to those considered appropriate to an officer; my behaviour would always have to be that considered suitable for an officer and from what I had seen of many WAAF Officers once they gained their Commission their accents, manner of speech and behaviour changed so much that many of them seemed to become really artificial people. I was just warming to my theme when the Assistant to the WAAF C.O. interjected "Pickering, we <u>are</u> hearing some home truths aren't we?" I have an idea that the interview did not go on long after that!

So now you will realise that my stupid insistence on telling the truth as I saw it was a very silly thing to do. In my childhood I had been told so often not to be so brusque and so insistent on being outspoken. I wonder what would have happened if I had been tactful instead of truthful? I cannot remember what I told my Mother about the interview – perhaps in this case I did "bend" the truth a wee bit so that her feelings would not be distressed by discovering once again how tactless her outspoken daughter could be.

6. *Kit inspections – on a charge*

Looking back to the days of my childhood I think that I have always had a tendency to be careless of the whereabouts of my possessions. When we lived at Saxilby, Hutson's bus, which used to take me to the dreaded Girls' High School in Lincoln, passed our house on the way to its turning point at "The Tree" near the Church before making its return journey to Lincoln. Seeing the red bus going up to "The Tree" used to give me a "five minute warning" to finish getting ready, run down the drive and hold up my hand for Mr. Hutson, or one of his drivers, to stop and pick me up opposite our house. I don't think that there were official bus stops in those days, certainly not at our end of the village.

During this five minute count down period pandemonium reigned as my Mother, and Grace our beloved maid, dashed around trying to find my mislaid possessions so that I could be bundled down the drive in order not to try Mr. Hutson's patience (and the accuracy of his timetable) by delaying his bus.

On numerous occasions I would bring the wrong book home for my homework. This upset me so much that my Mother and I would catch Mr. Hutson's bus once again, and go to Ruddock's Book Shop in Lincoln in order to try to purchase another copy. This did my Mother's housekeeping budget no good at all!

I have gone into my past like this in order to let you appreciate what a nightmare Kit Inspections were for me when I joined the WAAF and had to account for every single item that the Royal Air Force, in its generosity, had let me borrow.

Looking back I now realise that this feeling was probably the same for a number of other WAAF for, when the date of the dreaded Kit Inspection was announced, all those who realised an item of their kit was missing would seek to acquire a replacement wherever one was to be found. (The real owner's name marked on the kit was no deterrent to stop it being "'alf-inched"). The WAAF Officer inspecting usually counted that all the items were correct in number but I do not remember her ever checking if the names marked on them were correct.

In all my five years and eight days as a volunteer in the WAAF I was only on a Form 252 (Charge Sheet) just the once and it was all the result of a Kit Inspection that I had to suffer the gross indignity of being marched in to a WAAF Officer on a Charge of having Wilfully Lost (or words to that effect):

1 pair gloves, woollen, blue

1 scarf, woollen, blue

? a couple of under-garments (which defy description)

Now, I had a good alibi for the missing gloves and scarf. It so happens that one dark night I had been out with a friend when we heard metal crumpling and glass breaking and realised that not far away there had been an accident. So we hurried up the road to find a bus, which had crashed and some people were lying on the grass verge injured. It was an extremely dark night and we did what we could to help until the emergency services arrived to look after everyone.

I believe I lent my gloves and scarf and put my greatcoat over some of the injured, as it was a very cold night. Before leaving the site I remembered to retrieve my greatcoat and put it back on but forgot all about the scarf and gloves.

I told the WAAF Officer how I came to lose the scarf and gloves and she looked as though she doubted the veracity of my statement or, should I say, she thought I was "shooting a line". Fortunately I was able to point out to her a dried blood stain on the lapel of my greatcoat and I was believed.

I had no respectable alibi for my missing under-garments – which I still say had been taken by a person or persons un-known to make up their kit list. But how they came to lose them in the first place is not for me to conjure upon.

So I left the Charge Room without a stain on my character – only a stain on my greatcoat lapel – and a bill from Stores to replace the other missing garments.

Incidentally I am told that when a very small child I looked after a "possession" only too well – perhaps this little anec-dote will help to redress the balance concerning later carelessness with possessions.

As in many houses in the 1930s inside the front door stood a hat and coat stand with containers each side for walking sticks and umbrellas. In the middle there was a small, lidded wooden compartment for gloves etc.

I do not know where I found the darling little baby rabbit. It was definitely dead. I put it gently in the glove box amongst the gloves in the hat-stand, carefully covering it up with other gloves (no doubt some of them were rabbit-skin lined – so it should have felt as if it were at home down the burrow with the rest of the family). Presumably I felt I had done all that could be done for the poor little thing and soon forgot all about it.

In due course a strange, unfamiliar and unpleasant odour permeated our hallway – which no amount of "airing" could alleviate. In fact, it became worse. Much worse. The poor little body, which I had laid to rest so carefully was found amongst the gloves in the glove box. What happened next is buried in the past.

According to my letter home from Leicester Royal Infirmary in July 1942 I told my mother that in future we were to be issued with pyjamas. It seems that three months later two pairs were missing although they were marked with my name!

If only the WAAF Inspecting Officer had ever checked that the names on the kit matched the name of the person displaying it, the thefts would have been discovered and I should not have been charged for their replacement.

7. *More letters from Cottesmore; 1942*

Monday

Dearest,

As you may notice I got back quite safely on Saturday. It did not seem nearly so bad with the prospect of meeting Roo in Grantham – for a time I almost forgot that I was returning to Camp.

I managed to get a large Sorbo sponge at a chemists for 2/6d. It was the last one that they had so I was very lucky. If you will look out for a couple of soap containers I shall be very pleased.

This will probably be a very short note as the F/Lt is in the office and I may have to break off at any moment.

Was delighted to receive an Air Mail letter card (like the one I had before), from Les. It was only dated 7th January, so made very good time. It was evidently written during a bivouac on their advance, and he was evidently feeling very fed up. But glad to have received my Airgraph just previously, as it was the first news he had had of me since leaving England! Poor darling. I will quote you some of his letter:-

"Thanks awfully for your Airgraph received a few days ago. You cannot imagine how pleased I was to hear from you, and being as it was the first since leaving England you can well guess how very much it was appreciated."

I am glad to hear that you and your parents are in the best of health. That at least is one thing to be thankful for don't you think?

---------I shall not be in the least sorry when this little 'squabble' out here is over. How many times one longs for a little recreation such as

dancing or swimming – still the swimming may yet be possible at the rate we keep moving up, I should not be in the least surprised to find myself swimming in the 'Meddy' one of these mornings.

Please forgive writing. I'm writing this in a 'bivouac' that is hardly big enough to sit up in."

It was a very short letter, but I was very pleased to know that he was still O.K. a month ago, for except for the cable dated December I had not had a letter since about the end of November,

Love,

Sylvia

❖ ❖ ❖

426567 ACW/1 Pickering, S.

Station Armoury, R.A.F. COTTESMORE,

Wed. 7. Jan. 1942

Dearest One,

Sunday morning I had to come in to do P.T. before breakfast in the gym. It was ghastly, and I was so energetic in touching the floor with my hands flat on the ground instead of merely fingers, that I am consequently very stiff.

The day after was my day off and Roo and I decided (after much preamble and changing of minds) that we would go into Leicester for the day. So with a GREAT effort I got into Camp and had breakfast the same time as usual and met him at 9 o'clock! We walked down to Cottesmore and I simply had to call in and see Bridget and she came up and finished the remainder of a few toffees[1] that I had left from a previous occasion – I simply could not go away without giving her something, but it did hurt to give her those precious sweets, but she enjoyed them very much and asked for more.

---

[1] Sweets were rationed—so those given to Bridget could not easily be replaced.

We then walked about another ½ mile and got a lift in a small car to Oakham. I knew that as we intended to hitch hike to Leicester our best way would be to go via Uppingham. I had been to Uppingham (on my way to Kettering to see Vic) by bus, so I thought that I roughly knew the way. I started off the way I knew the bus had taken and we started to walk and we reached Uppingham about 1 o'clock!!!!!!¹

Apparently the way the bus had taken me was a long way round through small villages, so we started the first bit of the way on the bus route, then deviated from it, and then picked it up again before we got to Uppingham, so that was why I recognised part of the route and could not recognise the rest of the way. The proper way would have been about three miles nearer along a mainish road; we walked where No White Man Had Trod Before – almost anyway! Only two cars passed us in three hours!

However, we both enjoyed the walk, Roo especially as he is very fond of walking and it was a lovely day, bright and clear (with the wind behind us thank goodness), and very pretty hilly country streams etc., and we certainly found an appetite!

When we got to Uppingham we soon got a lift with a lorry load of baled hay into Leicester and then we set out for some food. Time 1.45 p.m.

Lewis's is really a marvellous shop, it had the most up-to-date things. We thought that it might be rather late to go upstairs for lunch in the Restaurant so when we saw a notice saying "Luncheonette" we decided to investigate. In the basement was set out a large space filled with small chairs and tables and a long servery all down one wall. Over it were such notices as Soda Fountain, Sandwich Bar, Fish Meals Here, Special Dinners Here etc. And according to what you wanted you went to the special counter dealing with it.

---

¹ All signposts had been removed so our way to Uppingham could not be checked by reference to them. This was supposed to puzzle the Germans if they landed—it certainly puzzled us!

We thought we would try a Special Dinner at 1/3d.[1] each. Excellent soup, Rissoles, carrots and mashed potato, and an enormous plate of rice pudding with raisins in, and a cup of tea to finish it up. I soon found that I was not as hungry as I thought I was!

After an excellent meal because, of course, I had to leave my pudding[2], I started to sample some of the other things – buns and a rich cream cake. We thought we would look round the rest of the shop and then go and see a film. I managed to get some Vanishing Cream of un-known make, which I am tentatively trying out on bits of me to see if it is Black Market before I put it on properly! And a lip stick re-fill, for I hear that cosmetics are going to be even more scarce in the Spring.

They even have escalators up to each of the four floors but the escala-tors only go upward! If you want to go <u>down</u> you either walk down the stairs or go by lift! The shop was really very like peace time and there seemed no shortage of toys and dolls either, 'tho I did not see the price on them.

After we had wandered round there for half an hour our legs began to feel a trifle weary once more and we bought a local paper and decided to go and see George Formby in "South American George". It was a very modern cinema and we thoroughly enjoyed it, because of course, it was most amusing.

When we came out it was quite dark and we thought it would be best to verify the time of the train back to Oakham for I knew that there always used to be one at 9.15. Apparently there are several stations in Leicester and I did not know whether Oakham was L.N.E.R. or L.M.S. First of all we were directed to one that seemed deserted and no signs of life anywhere – I don't know whether it was disused or merely that it is not used after black-out time, but it was no use to us, so we went back to the centre of the town again.

Eventually we found the station and that the train still ran at 9.15 so we went back into Town to look for somewhere to eat and had some

---

[1] Equivalent to 6.25 pence

[2] I don't like milk puddings

tea-supper. The train was quite crowded and so we helped ourselves to a 1st class carriage where we were joined by some more people and then everybody made themselves as comfortable as possible and went to sleep. Or so it seemed. One soldier did snore!

Next day I looked up on the map where we had been and found where we had gone wrong and measured our route on a 1 inch to 1 mile map. It was two miles to where we had got our lift to Oakham. 8½ miles from Oakham to Uppingham and I should think that we walked a further three miles in search of the station, shop-gazing etc. A total of 13½ miles! I must say we were a bit stiff the next day, 'tho not so tired as I would have expected. I am sure the fresh air and exercise did me a world of good!

I have started to take up fencing, which is an extremely energetic pursuit, of which I will tell you more later. (P.T. plus walk to Leicester, plus fencing and Dance to follow you can imagine what my leg muscles feel like to-day). Will you please, as soon as possible, cut off the top of my gym tunic and turn it into a skirt for me – it will be absolutely ideal, for a skirt is too tight and it is so nicely pleated. If you are too busy to do it at once will you please press my shorts and send them.

After fencing I went to the Camp Dance with Vic and was too stiff to dance much so ate five Choc ices instead!

love and hugs from

Bunty

❖   ❖   ❖

426567 ACW/1 Pickering, S.

Station Armoury

(undated) January, 1942

Dearest One,

I shall not be coming home on Saturday or at the beginning of next week for several reasons. I cannot get off early enough to come with

Mary who starts her "48" on Saturday, for the W.O.[1] is going on a '48' at that time and the F/Sgt and F/Lt both have Sunday off so it would mean that there was nobody in either of the offices. Even if they were not going to be away I very much doubt if my pass would have gone through in time.

We got back quite comfortably on Tuesday, when we got into Grantham we went into the Milk Bar and then a Canteen. I had a glass of Horlicks and a Welsh rarebit and thanks so much for the cakes too! I am sure that you will think my appetite quite O.K.

Roo went down to Sick Bay yesterday for something for his cold and they took his temperature and found it 98.8° – he tried to blow on it, shake it and get it down but the Med. Orderlies prevented him, and they have detained him for 24 hrs. His great friend Jack Kean came in to tell me, unfortunately the F/Lt and another officer were in the office when Jack came and I was very afraid the F/Lt would turn round and want to know what it was all about.

So that as we were unable to go out I thought it would be a good opportunity to go back to the Hall and get some work done. I made Mary's and my beds, cleaned buttons and shoes; emptied the pockets of my best blues and hung them up; darned two pairs of stockings, washed 1 pr stockings, knickers, linings and brassiere and then had a good wash myself and managed to be in bed by 9.30 p.m.

I have just been to dinner and saw Roo standing outside the Sgts. Mess with some other Australians, he waved and appears to be O.K.

To-night is our domestic evening when we polish our floors, dust, sweep and are supposed to mend our clothes. So to-night I hope to mend my 'black-outs' and sew my "A's" on my greatcoat, also re-sew the wings for they have nearly come off. By then I expect it will be soon after nine and I shall go to sleep – or I should perhaps say try to sleep as with everyone in it will not be easy.

---

[1] W.O.—Warrant Officer

To-morrow, Friday, I expect Roo and I will go into Oakham to see "Major Barbara". I have heard that it is well worth seeing, and as Wendy Hiller of Pygmalion fame is in it I expect that I shall enjoy it.

On Saturday Tubby (from North Luffenham with whom I travelled on leave) has invited me to meet him in Oakham and have a chat and something to eat. Perhaps he will give me a lesson in snooker which he has promised to do if I want to learn.

Sunday night there is our Dancing class so you will know where I am when you happen to think of me.

with lots of love from

Bunty

426567 ACW/1 Pickering, S.

Station Armoury, R.A.F. COTTESMORE, Rutland

26th January, 1942

Dearest One,

I have rushed my 7 day's leave in for Saturday, and I hope it will come through for it is supposed to always be in at least ten days before one wants to go. I thought that it would be no good saving up for a fortnight later on for you won't be able to get 14 days at a time now.

I shall probably be coming altogether by myself, as Roo came in yesterday to tell me that in all probability he will be posted next week. That was a great shock, for he was expected to be here for another couple of months, but apparently they have too many Courses on the Station owing to the flying programme being held up by the weather and his is one of the names to go. Nothing definite is known as yet, but he is going to try hard and get a '48' before he goes, but is not very hopeful of it.

All being well, and if I get an early chit, I shall be home around tea time on Saturday, whoopee!

I was very pleased to receive a Cable from Les. dated 29th December in which he said that he was safe and well. In What the Stars Foretell it said that I would receive news from abroad this week, so the stars must have known it was on the way!

So far Bridget seems to be weathering the winter very well, and doesn't appear to be miserable. When there was deep snow on the ground she had plenty of hay, and was nuzzling her way down to the grass through the snow in quite the approved fashion. I nearly said like Peter used to do, but it still hurts too much to make that simile, and it will be a very long time indeed before I forgive her.

I went down last night with Roo before the Dancing class to see her but don't think that she had been fed. Perhaps they thought she did not need any now that the snow has gone, but I think that I shall ask them to give her some every day no matter what the weather. I must ask Ivy to send the haynet into Lincoln, for her hay was blowing about all over the snow and it was such a waste.

Poor Mrs. Penn![1] Really, Toomai[2] is a little mischief, when Mrs. Penn ran away I expect he said to himself: 'So you won't play huh!' I hope that you got 2d. for its tail!

Will not write more now, but will look forward instead to telling you it all on Saturday and the ensuing days!

Lots and lots of love and mush from,

Bunty

---

[1] Our neighbour.

[2] Our cat. Presumably Toomai took a rat he had killed to Mrs. Penn; she could claim 2d. on it which was the "Bounty" given for each rat tail during the war.

426567 Lac Pickering, S.

Station Armoury, R.A.F. COTTESMORE, Rutland

27th March, 1942 0850 hours Friday

My Dearest One,

I hope I can get a good deal of this letter written before the F/Lt comes in. He usually arrives about 9.15. I think that it would be a good idea if you addressed me as Lac instead of Lacw and see what happens. At present they always note the 'w' in my address and send it to the W.A.A.F. Guard Room. If you sent it as Lac, it would look as if it was a R.A.F. and it would be delivered to the Section.

Gee, it is lucky that I remembered to put in the day for I had quite forgotten that it was Friday and Pay Day! Last Pay Day was also my day off, and I have not bothered to put in a chit for casual payment since. So all being well I should get a month's pay to-day which will be very nice. I shall then be able to send you the money for the stamp collection, for I have already settled up Bridget's account.

They really are marvellous people. Roo and I went to settle up on Saturday after the hockey match and before the concert. Mrs. Fountain was only in at first, and we did not know how much was to be charged for her hay (she had quite a lot during the snow, for I have seen her there with more than she could bother to eat for the time being). I had already 6/- in credit and had to pay for all the time since last January, so I said I would leave £3 and they could tell me what it was afterwards. Just as I was leaving Mr. Fountain came in and insisted that I took £1 back, which I thought was perfectly marvellous of them, don't you? They are also going to get her taken to the blacksmith's for me to have her shoes removed, so I should be able to do some riding soon. My breeches are awaiting collection at the cleaner's, 'tho as she is so scruffy it seems a pity that I shall have to ride in my best ones.

I don't seem to be able to get on very well with this letter but I have to go on Parade in the morning now, so do not have so much time, and 20 mins. walk before lunch.

<u>1610 hours</u> It has been another lovely day to-day, 'tho' the wind is rather cold. Roo is flying this afternoon but hopes to return in time to go into Oakham this evening, for he will be flying to-morrow night and we shall not be able to go out then.

To-morrow afternoon I am playing in a hockey match at 2.30 against Ashwell Camp. I had thought that it was a Match against the A.T.S. but to my horror have found it is a Mixed Match, for there are only 5 W.A.A.F. on our side plus a reserve! So think of poor little me among the Army Boots. I am going to ask the F/Lt if I can have my pads armour-plated!

I had a letter from Di yesterday with some rather surprising news. Their house is to be used for a Land Army hostel and they have to move out by the 6th April. According to Di it seems to have come rather suddenly, but they have got another farm near Bourne.

By the way, I <u>did</u> manage to get a lot of letters written when I was on duty, in spite of the fact that I was longing to read some of the books with which Roo had provided me. I wrote to Tubby, Vic, Mary Stevens and most important of all, to you. Actually the evening did not seem so long as I thought it would, 'tho I know that if I had started to read instead of write I should have gone to sleep for sure.

I have had a very satisfactory pay day to-day – for a month, as I did not go last time – £4.10s. so can send you our stamp money. I think it would be safer to register it, but will not send it with this letter as it may take several days to reach you, and I want you to have a letter a day if possible either from Roo or me.

Roo has just passed the window and held his hand up to indicate 5 o'clock so that means the five o'clock bus and tea in Oakham which will be a very pleasant change.

So for now darling, au revoir, and God bless

Loads of love from little

Me

426567 Lac Pickering, S.

Station Armoury, R.A.F. COTTESMORE, Rutland

Saturday, 28th March, 1942

My Dearest darling,

I was very relieved to get your letter this morning and to know that everything is satisfactory and you are not feeling too bad.

I also had an Airgraph from Les. this morning dated 19th February so things have speeded up a bit. He did not give much news but referred to bits in my letters and was delighted because he had 3 letters from me in three weeks. That reminds me I must send him another. He wishes that I told him we collected stamps before, for he has had many opportunities some time ago, but will do the best he can for us.

I cannot think of much other news so will tell, rather belatedly, of our day off last Monday. It was a particularly nice one because I did not have to get up early like I usually do on our day's off when we want to go anywhere, but this time we did not want to do too much walking about as I was so stiff from hockey.

I slept right through everyone getting up (a thing I have never done before), and woke up at 8.0 but slept again 'till nine when I got up and had a bath. Owing to the laundry not having arrived for several weeks I had not got a bath towel so took up with me an old shirt, a pair of nice cottony linings and a large clean hankie of Roos. Unfortunately I found the shirt did not dry at all well, and struck very cold, the pants were by far the best! And did not have to use the hankie!

I was out by 10.15 and started on the 1½ mile walk to Cottesmore where we intended to catch the bus. Roo said he would walk out to meet me, and as I was a quarter of an hour later than I had intended, only had to walk just out of sight of the Hall and there he was sitting on a tree trunk waiting for me. He had seen a squirrel too, which is more than I have done there.

We were lucky enough to get a lift into Cottesmore in a car, and then easily caught the bus. We found the train did not go until 11.30 so had ¾ hr. to wait. It hardly seemed worth while walking back into *the town, so we thought that we would <u>see</u> if we could get some cider, for it was very cold on the station, of course we were unsuccessful, but had a very nice grapefruit instead and sat by the fire reading a Tatler (or similar magazine) of the year 1919 A.D. The clothes were really astounding!!*

The run into Nottingham takes 1¼ and when we got there our first thought was lunch, but about the first thing that caught my eye was a notice advertising a circus. As you know, I have not seen one for years, and Roo had never seen one at all, so I thought that it was my duty to edify him, so we, or should I say <u>I</u> decided we would go.

First of all we had lunch in an exclusive, and rather expensive restaurant. We were so hungry that we could not be bothered to look any further, 'tho it had very nice surroundings of oak panelled walls and large brass embossed trays and shields on the walls. The place was called King's Restaurant and is about at right-angles to the Town Hall.

After lunch we went and queued to book our seats for the Circus and then went shop gazing for the remainder of the afternoon. We were exploring Woolworth's and discovered that they had a very nice basement café place, with tables and chairs etc. We did not seem to have seen many cafes so we stayed there and had some excellent fish and chipped potatoes. Followed by, guess what ------ 4½ tiny meringues! Believe you me, we are going to Nottingham again even if it is only to see if they have got any left!

It was then time to go to our Circus which was a show lasting 1¾ hrs. The people were a great deal better than the animals with the exception of the elephants. I will include the programme – which <u>sounds</u> good – for your interest.

I never noticed Item 1.

No. 2 was feeble.

3. was very clever, a board balanced on a roller on a table on which he danced. In the end Vivienne climbed up on his shoulders too – it certainly was a good bit of balance.

4.   *I don't know if Billy was malaise, but only Betsy appeared. I imagine Billy was sulking, for Betsy was not at all happy and did most of her tricks with her ears laid back and lashed out at him in an exasperated way several times. Except for making them lie down, which is quite easy, Peter[1] had a thousand times more brain and intelligence and he did his tricks happily. Bless him.*

5.   *I had never seen wire walking before, and it was marvellous.*

6.   *The bear looked positively moth-eaten, and all it did was come on the stage, beg, roll over on its back and drink out of a bottle. 'Astonishing bear' indeed, astonishingly poor show.*

7.   *I can't make out why the Pekinese had the name 'performing' for all it did was to jump over a series of low hurdles – Punch[2] was more clever.*

8.   *Amusing.* 9. *A very good show, but how the floor of the stage bore the weight of the two elephants I don't know.*

10.   *Excellent.* 11.   *Lousy – 'tho did look a little happier, all they did was trot round in circles and change direction on command.*

13.   *Knife throwing and lassoeing.* 14. *Nothing special, only good balance and agility.*

15.   *A good bit of clowning.*

16.   *Quite good, for the lions certainly did give the impression of being very fierce, 'tho I always think it looks rather degrading to see a lion doing tricks.*

The ones I marked with a red cross were really good though. And I suppose I am naturally critical as regards animals, for I probably know more about them than the average circus-goer.

We had some time to wait before the train so looked for cider again at a very nice old fashioned hotel, – complete with most austere butler. Unsuccessful but had two very nice limes instead. The first since I was

---

[1] Peter—my first pony

[2] Punch—my wire haired terrier

introduced to them in Malta at Dickie Douglas's when we went there during the 'gregale.'

Must stop, will miss post

love from

Bunty

426567 Lacw Pickering, S.

R.A.F. Cottesmore

8.15 a.m. Wed. 24th June, 1942

My Darling,

... I am going to make an effort to write to you on Sundays and Wednesdays like I used to do at Boarding School. I don't know how long this good resolution will last but I can but try. So far I have written a letter a day – Saturday a p.c. to you, Sunday a letter to you, Monday one to Uncle E.W., yesterday morning to Tubby and last night to Roo. At this rate (if I keep it up) I should have a few letters coming in soon.

... Roo went back on the 7.30 bus with Jackass[1] and I went back to the Hall at 8.30 and then to bed. By the way, I have just remembered that I cannot fasten my skirt owing to the lack of a big button and some press studs or hooks and eyes, could you please try and find the necessary? It is rather urgent.

---

[1]At my sister's farm at Leadenham there appeared a small, hungry stray dog like a wire-haired terrier. We nicknamed him "Jackass". Roo said he would take him back to Camp with him and try to keep him as a pet. If they were doing exercises below the need for oxygen I believe Jackass sometimes went with the crew. It is not known what happened to Jackass. He finally disappeared at the same time as another crew with whom he was friendly did not return.

Apparently while I was away[1] the Fountain's were very short of grass and wanted me to move Bridget. Roo went down to see them next day to ask Mr. F. if he could suggest anywhere else for me to enquire so that he could go round and fix things up for me. In the end Mr. Fountain said that she can stay until the end of September but he will not be able to have her this winter. Do you think they would be able to have her at Leadenham? Roo said that Mr. F. thought that it was a pity she was not in foal for he thought she would have a good one – that was without Roo mentioning the subject[2]. Roo offered him some more for her keep but it seemed only to be the grass shortage which had been worrying him, but I shall either go down or write and offer him another shilling a week.

I have just rung up W.A.A.F. Sick Quarters to see if the M.O. has said anything about sending me to Rauceby to see an ENT Specialist – but as I thought, he was intending to wait until I was ill again to prove that they really were troubling me, so I am going down again today to beard him in his den and try and get something done.

Poor S/Ldr has had a terrible time whilst I have been away. 'Where were you when we had the busiest two months we have ever had?' 'Five weeks Sir'. 'Two months.' 'No, only five weeks Sir'. 'It was two months, and you can tell your Mother that she won't see you home again for at least a year. There was I filing letters right and left, having to do all my letters by hand – and where were you?!' So I told him that he should appreciate me now. Yesterday he was asking how I felt, and whether I thought I should crock up again. I said that I certainly hoped I shouldn't. Whereat he laughed most heartily and said 'YOU hope not, YOU hope not – what about ME? So I think that he must have missed me after all. He really is a dear.

---

[1] I was away for five weeks with tonsillitis and bronchitis

[2] By the following year I was at R.A.F. Coningsby; Bridget was with me—and a marriage was arranged for her and she duly had a son.

By the way, what am I going to do on my day off, for I should be too stiff if I rode Bridget for long. Could I ring up Harold[1] and see if he would meet me in Grantham for lunch? After all he is a cousin...

426567 Lacw Pickering S,

R.A.F. Cottesmore

28th June, 1942

Dearest,

To-day is the W.A.A.F's birthday – its 3rd. This morning we had a big parade of 200 of the W.A.A.F. and were inspected by the W.A.A.F. and R.A.F. C.O. it was really quite fine. Then we went to the Station Church and had a nice little sermon – quite a jolly morning.

Tonight we are having a Dance to which we can invite Sgts and F/Sgts! The first time that we have ever been allowed to invite anyone above the rank of Cpl and now that I have been away for five weeks I don't know anyone – the first time for nine months. I am told that we are going to have a marvellous feed including ice cream, trifles and a big birthday cake so shall go for the eats. Each W.A.A.F. is allowed to invite one person, but I am told that S/Ldr Robertson has invited an extra course of Sgts so there is just a chance that I may be able to find someone there to amuse myself with.

Dora Williams set my hair for me with some setting lotion last night and it looks wizard this morning although it had not been washed first and was a trifle greasy. Little curls at the back, up the sides and curls on top. An unheard of thing happened this morning S/Ldr said 'Who did your hair this morning?' And he never hardly remarks on anything.

---

[1] Harold—New Zealand cousin whom I met when he was training at R.A.F. Cottesmore

I went to German class on Thursday night and got on fairly well. The class has been going since about Easter but have not got too advanced yet provided that I do a bit of revision.

Thank you very much for the press studs etc. You have no idea how urgently they were required.

Lots of love, Bunty

Memories of S/Ldr Johnson, Station Armament Officer

R.A.F. Woolfox Lodge was an airfield used by R.A.F. Cottesmore until August 1941. It was situated about six miles south of Stamford on the eastern side of the Great North Road (A1). The enemy had dropped some bombs on the airfield which had not exploded. S/Ldr Johnson asked if I would like to accompany him as a change from the office. I gladly accepted. We drove across the airfield but stopped some distance from where fluttering red flags stuck in the ground showed where the bombs were. My boss invited me to walk across with him to have a close-up look at them, being a coward, I thanked him and declined his invitation saying "There'll never be another me!" He seemed surprised and continued alone.

Once I was offered a great South African treat – Biltong, a narrow strip of meat, salted and sun dried but it was not to my taste.

This is a photo of preparations being made for a bomb-ing-trip to Bremen on 25th/26th June, 1942. This was one of the "1,000

bomber raids" when, in order to make up the number, some not fully trained crews from O.T.U's were included. S/Ldr Johnson is on the right. Mike Garbett tells me the Armourers are fitting bomb racks capable of holding small bombs (250 lbs.)

Occasionally I was asked to leave our shared office as he wished to don a fencing mask as a safety precaution to deal with a detonator or something like that. If anything went wrong I should not be in the danger zone!

He was scrupulously fair. When he was the Mess Secretary he asked if I would mind accompanying him to the Officers' Mess to do a little typing there but pointed out that it was up to me to choose whether or not to do so as it was not one of my WAAF duties. Of course, I went.

Whilst working for S/Ldr Johnson my annual Proficiency Assessment was given by him as "Exceptional". Needless to say, I never rose to such heights again.

8. *To Leicester Royal Infirmary*

I imagine that I should have gone into Rauceby R.A.F. Hospital to have my tonsils removed, but as my mother was a friend of Miss Marriott, the Matron of Leicester Royal Infirmary, it was arranged that I should go there instead. In a letter dated 31st July, 1942 Miss Marriott wrote to my Mother saying I had had "my very nasty septic embedded tonsils removed" and that "this afternoon Mr. Kendall came in to see her and said that she was going on well. Expect she will be going to Peatling Parva Hall early next week, that is one of the Service Convalescent places. It is a nice place, have been once or twice when doing Regional Inspections."

Peatling Parva Hall (photo by Leslie Watts 1999)

I duly went to Peatling Parva Hall to convalesce but felt rather an "outsider" as no other WAAF were there. The Hall lay well away down a slope from the quiet lane in the wee village of Peatling Parva, right in the depths of the Leicestershire countryside. I believe that twice a week a bus ran to Leicester.

One of the A.T.S. girls was a real "townie" and the peace and tranquillity of the place irked rather than soothed her. She longed for the hustle and bustle of people and the noise of unceasing traffic. She told us she would run away. We did not believe her. One day she was discovered to be missing and then there was a great hue and cry to try and find her. But we, the "inmates", were never told the end of this "Great Escape". It was certainly the most memorable happening during my pleasant stay at Peatling Hall!

Saturday, L.R.I.

July, 1942

Dearest Mummy,

Thank you so much for your two letters, I have had a wonderful lot of letters (you must have done a lot of canvassing darling) including: Harold (1), Roo including a parcel of chocs, Auntie Margery, Bay, Elsie, Tubby, Mary Wood, Ivy and I can't remember who else, anyway the day before yesterday it was six letters, yesterday five and a parcel and today three. Better than a birthday!

I am feeling a lot better now and I get up to get washed etc.

Dear old Doc Kendall came in yesterday afternoon and held my hand and told me that I shall probably be going to Peatling Parva or wherever it is on Monday, so you better go straight home and not tire yourself by making detours.

On Wednesday I had a visitor Brenda Tilley (not Acres). She told me she would call in if she came to Leicester. The next day another one came from our room. I can't think of her name at the moment. She brought me a lovely bunch of sweet peas, so you see I have been very lucky.

They say that even if I do go to P. Parva it will not count as sick leave, and when I get back to camp I shall still be merely "Discharged from Hospital" and should still have sick leave to come. Otherwise I think I shall brave the S/Ldr for a week's leave for I am longing to be home again and dying to see the rabbits.

By the way, before I forget – Pyjamas. You will not need to get me any because they are now going to be issued to us. I knew that the chit was not valid, as people couldn't use chits for things after about April, but I wondered if you knew anyone well enough who could wangle.

Since I wrote the last bit I have had a nice long nap but feel very bleary in consequence.

Well, there's one good thing, as they were exceptionally bad tonsils I should be very noticeably better in the future. Harold[1] tells me to watch out, for when he had his out he gained 1st. 13lbs. and grew 4 inches in 12 months and wonders if I should do the same! Gosh, I hope not. I was so pleased to get his letter, and it was such a surprise, but he said you had told him.

He has done a tremendous amount of flying, night and day since his leave, incl. 3 ops trips and was on another Thurs night. That means he should have not more than six to do, I think, before he has finished.

He asked me to tell you he had received the Polyfotos[2] Earlier he said " – your tonsils out. Poor kid, never mind,......" I am sure he thinks I must be a very juvenile cousin to look up to his lofty seniority. He was sorry he could not get over to see me, but hopes to manage it when I get home – "it is full moon time" now.

---

[1] My New Zealand cousin

[2] Similar to booth style passport photographs

This writing paper is a farce. I picked up a chunk out of the office and thought it was my usual quality but only the outside sheets were O.K. but I thought you wouldn't mind.

It is a great relief to be able to talk more easily. Daddy wouldn't understand how I have managed all this time!

Will send you my new address as soon as I know it. You certainly did have a hectic time, <u>do</u> take care of yourself.

Oodles of love to you and all at Sutton, especially to Aunt Lily.

Bunty

P.S. Enclose an envelope – pity to waste it.

A letter from my New Zealand cousin Harold:

> *408 Squadron,*
>
> *Balderton*
>
> *Thursday*

Dear Bunty,

Had a letter from Aunty saying you are in hospital having your tonsils out. Poor Kid, never mind, it will be a good job done and I hope it is all over now and that you are well on the way to recovery.

Sorry I was unable to get up to see you last Saturday, but we have been chasing our tails round so hard here that we are positively giddy. I have done three operational trips since being back from leave and am on another tonight. This is besides all the day flying we have been doing, and believe you me, we have been doing some. I wish I could get down to see you, but it is no good wishing, because I know I won't have a chance.

How long do you think you will be there? I suppose you will have some time at home before you go back to Cottesmore, I should get a chance to hop up and see you then.

Watch out young Lady, I put on 1 stone 13 lbs when I had my tonsils out in 12 months and grew 4 inches, that is the truth, its no lie, but I was a growing boy at the time, 14 years to be exact. You're a fully matured woman? so you are okay??

Darned tease aren't I, all the same I hope you are well on the way to recovery and your old self and not feeling any after effects.

Hoping to see you during your convalescence.

Until then Yours with love,

Harold

P.S. Tell Aunty Betty, I got the Polyfotos okay, and what photos, like a page out of a comic paper. I'll bring it with me when I come. H.

Sunday, 2.9.42

Dearest Poppet,

So sorry that you have been a bit longer than usual without a letter. I thought that I would probably have told you that I was taking Bridget over yesterday and that I might have seen you there. But it would not really have been worth it, as I did not get there until about 3.30 and had to leave again at 6.45.

Next weekend I <u>hope</u> to arrange it so that I can get over for Sturton Show, please confirm that it is on that date for I don't want to make a mistake about the date. Also what time it begins. For I shall need to know in order to try and arrange it so that I can be there, for usually I am not home for an afternoon and evening. May have my pass from 11.30 a.m. to 11.30 a.m. the next day if that would get me home in time and the S/Ldr agrees. I do certainly want to be there if I can possibly manage. it.

By the way, Mrs. Potts our W.A.A.F. Asst/Adjt says that a W.A.A.F. Officer A/S/O[1] gets about as much as a clerk Cpl when the messing bills etc. are knocked off it. Gee!

---

[1] A/S/O—Assistant Section Officer (lowest rank for a WAAF officer)

I had rather a tiring ride yesterday, and am ghastly stiff to-day, never have been so stiff in my life before I am thinking.

Poor Biddy she was tired too and by the time that we got to Ancaster must have looked a miserable pair – she walking slowly along with her head down and loose reins, me with feet out of stirrups, hand on the pommel to prop myself up and eyes shut!

However, I think that she is jolly clever, for when we were just beyond Byard's Leap she recognised where she was and did not half brighten up and knew all the rest of the turnings to Leadenham and intended that I should make no mistake about them either! even managed a fast canter – before she had only done a slow walk or an amble or a trot! She did not get a very welcome reception, but I hope that they will be good enough to keep her for me to the end of the winter.

Bay says that she thinks she would like to buy Snow White[1] if you want to sell her.

No time for more now darling, or else I shall miss the post, looking forward to seeing you next weekend.

Lots of love from your own, Bunty

---

[1] The rabbit

9.   *Roo Is On Ops*

The following letters were written when Roo was on operational duties flying as a Navigator in 97 Lancaster Bomber Squadron from R.A.F. Woodhall Spa, close to R.A.F. Coningsby, to which I should be posted in February 1943 after the death of my mother.

The letters are undated. Some were written before I had my "very nasty septic tonsils" removed at Leicester Royal Infirmary in July, 1942 or when I was convalescing afterwards at Peatling Parva Hall in Leicestershire and others when I was back on duty at Cottesmore when Roo was fatherly in his insistence that I took better care of my health.

Walter "Roo" Langworthy

I was told "on the grapevine" that the strain of operational flying was taking its toll. Diary entries on 8th October, 1942 and 17th October, 1942 seem to agree with this. Ellie, his wife, wanted to know why his letters to her seemed strange and cold. He wanted to tell her about his affection for me. I told him not to do so. I did not want her to be upset by the news that I existed. Roo had barely a 50/50 chance of coming through the war alive anyway. At the beginning of our friendship I had told Roo that I would never come between a man and his wife, no matter how I felt, and that he should write Ellie a loving letter and tell her that he was suffering a lot of stress from flying on ops. When we were able to meet and be together, we would live for the day only, and not think about what the future held for us. I think he must have done this for in one of his letters he said "I can even write love letters.... – and if you keep your tongue in your cheek 'tis marvellous what you can do – so you ask me to live in the present, well the present contains you... so I guess I can, but don't be surprised if I break down sometimes – after all I'm not a machine... Guess we'll take the present and make it <u>OURS</u>. Can <u>YOU</u>..."

I do not know what would have happened if Roo had not been married. I knew he was "forbidden territory". I would never let myself be the cause of a divorce, no matter how much it hurt always to say "NO!" I supported him as much as I could by regularly writing, as he said my letters meant a great deal to him. But I knew his talk of a honeymoon in Tasmania and a holiday in Adelaide – both of which he was sure I would enjoy, would never come about.

Goodness knows why he thought "I had played him for a sucker". Presumably things between us were amicably sorted out for he turned up at Saxilby and attended my Mother's funeral in February, 1943. After the service we left everyone at the graveside and went off together on a long walk before he caught the bus back to Lincoln and then on to Woodhall Spa to continue operational flying. I explained that the death of my mother left me feeling alone and vulnerable and I should want to lean on him for support. This I must not do. Therefore, I would not see him again until I felt strong enough not to give in to my feelings towards him. This was a terribly hard decision for me to make. Half of me said "Yield". The other half said "You must NOT give in". We parted. Never to meet again.

Somewhere is an unopened letter I wrote to Roo in early 1943 explaining that I then felt strong enough to be in contact with him again. It was returned to me by the G.P.O. I believe it was marked "MISSING" so that is why I believed Roo was dead.

Camp, Sunday

Beloved,

Just a few lines before we take off the rest to be finished when we return and sent on to you tomorrow. I wish I knew when you were coming out of the convalescent home dearest. Don't know why but I've felt deucedly low today – very in fact – guess its the weather, but more likely the fault lies with me not seeing you for such a long time. It is a long long time. It is a long time darling, the worst spell we've ever had and I wish – oh –

I hope you're feeling O.K. now dear and that the throat is almost back to normal once more. It shouldn't take long now if everything has gone along according to plan, but of course you never can tell and my Rabbit – well – she's something special and so she will look after herself and not go trying dangerous experiments with various kinds of foods, or try exercising the vocal cords on Top C.

Devine and self are buying a wireless set between us to while away the hours at night – er – when we get any free nights – so with wireless and cat – beg pardon miaow – kitten we should be quite a domesticated pair for the bachelors ball what! Last night we spent putting up the aerial. Our kite had the aerial shot away t'other night and so we got the remains and its doing – or rather going to do service. We spent fully an hour trying out various positions for it but at last we decided the best place for it was from the EL standard on top of the Lav – to a tree (nearly said gum tree) so as I'd managed to climb and scramble on top of the lav. roof (not bad for my age really) we had to scale the tree and swing it over a limb. We then shot off at right angles and brought it over to our chimney, so I had a second scramble up over the roof this time – much more pleasant odour really – this took us 2½ hours, so we did a thorough job. We then decided to hold fast and have a rest before putting in the earth. We just got this started when down came the rain. So that earth is still in the makings. The lads in the W/T section are putting the final touches to the set tonight so we'll collect same when we come back from ops. Doesn't seem a bad set really – but of course we'll know more when we get it going.

Well cherie there's no sign of any leave on just yet. The W/Cdr threw a scare into us today when he yelled for our crew except the pilot – to stand by as he wanted us – 'Twas to be a daylight – but thank goodness it was scrubbed – Wasn't worried about that part of it – but didn't fancy navigating for the Winko – still. However we're doing the trip on our own. Seems to be something in the air tho'. Saw the Yankee kites the Fortresses flying in formation tonight and we've been detailed to stand ready for high level work – so we may at last be going to do something really good to shake the German brutes. Enuf of this dope –

Now dearest I guess you'll be heading for home in another day or so and I hope you do get at least 7 days sick leave. I hope I'll be able to see something of you then – but I really don't know how I stand as far as your mother is concerned. However you'll give me all particulars when you're going etc. etc. etc. – and there's such a lot to tell you – I'll be so glad darling when you do get out of that ....???..... and to some place where I can at least get to you if only for an hour or so. Three weeks yesterday – what a time. No wonder I've been feeling blue – but darling I certainly miss you. You give me that – oh – here I go again –

Cheerio for now dearest. Do you know anything about TOPS, and I do dearest honestly 100% as always. I'll enclose a brief note when I get back just to let you know everything's O.K.

All my love dearheart. I do hope you're feeling almost on top of the world again.

Yours, Roo

Same Place, Sunday

Dearest One,

Just a brief line to catch the mail – have just arrived back after being diverted all over England the last 3 days. Let me start – Last Friday we went to Genoa and had quite a good trip – incidentally we got diverted on the way back to Tangmere on the S. Coast – and couldn't take off back to our 'drome till Monday afternoon. Just had time to make up your parcel and rush off down to briefing again – We're off on a trip to the Baltic – Hell of a trip – Seemed to rush into everything – on the way over and what with diving about and swerving I got quite brassed off and felt somewhat sick – not that I was. To make matters worse – we ran over a Jerry convoy and wow! for a time we did some tight turns and dives as we were down at about 800 ft. ready to drop our mines. However we put our nose down and were "gone with the wind!" – we had to circle and do our run again – T'wasn't very pleasant but had to be – we dropped them O.K. Hope the convoy fell for them – we then set off for home – got back over base and were diverted to Leconfield. We couldn't get away from that darned place for 2 days – Wed. and Thurs.

Friday we set off for home unshaven, unwashed, untoothcleaned etc. – and found we were on last night. We had to take up our kite[1] for an N.F.T.[2] and couldn't land at base again so had to go to Scampton. Hell, were we wild. Nice Italian trip all in the bag and we had to miss it. We spent the night at Scampton not very much washed or shaved. In fact I had to put in a new blade to cut the bristles away when I arrived back here.

Found your letter in the rack this morn., the first time I've been in the Mess since last week – so fortunately I couldn't worry over whether you were O.K. or not – but guessed you were. We get a spot of leave from A/D[3] Thursday I think. What do you say, pet. I wonder if you could get a 48 or not.

Don't think I'll stay on the camp at Cottesmore – had enough of camp for a while. Haven't left the darned place except for the diversions since last leave – had thought I might look up my people in Devon and Cornwall – before venturing to Lancashire – but don't fancy turning up and saying "I'm me! You're you". Write back and let me know what you suggest – perhaps you can figure out something – but remember I'm pretty dull y'know – and now that I've been camp bound so long my ever so "witty" conversation is extra dull – so I guess I'll not be so very entertaining. Still, we'll see what you suggest when you write. Glad you liked the oranges – thought you would.

Glad you're improving so much in your dancing... You'll soon be able to earn extra money after the war as a professional dancer à la Pavlova – still you have a competent teacher.

Oh by the bye – would it be too much trouble to draw out that £sd[4] for me? Forgot Xmas was so near. Will have to send home money as a Xmas present and that would help without draining my present stock too much.

---

[1] (slang) an aeroplane

[2] Night Flying Test

[3] After Duty

[4] I took care of some of Roo's pay. If he went missing I was to keep it.

Write back straight away and let me know what you think. Yes life is rather grand isn't it. Marvellous what a break in world affairs does to one's outlook after so much stalemate.

Cheerioh for now. T.J.C. was <u>very</u> pleased to see us – she had been on iron rations for quite a while – in fact she is quite operationally minded – sometimes annoyed when her meals aren't regular. So nice of the Dear Old Lad to remember me. Ye Gods, charming. A mistake somewhere, what! Look after yourself and don't get that cold.

Love, Roo

Same Place, Friday Morn

Dearest One,

Horror of horrors – I've developed the awfully bad policy of talking in my sleep – or so Andy informs me. I take a very dim view of that, you know – you never know what secrets of your inner-self are revealed – but as there is only Tweedles and Andy to hear is not as bad. I hope I never let out anything of importance – tis all rather relative isn't it. Never know I might give away the secrets of the Lancaster – and there would be Tweedles dressed up in a W.A.A.F. uniform – wouldn't she look smart with a swastika painted on her side. Think I'll peroxide her just to see – doing the goose – er – cat step up to old Hitler and in her mewing tongue telling him all about it. Dear dear – what it is to have a woman in the hut. S'awful – here she is sitting up on my knees and feeling quite at home. Did I tell you we've had to cut her claws. Most decidedly. She was ripping everything up including us – but somehow I don't think we made a very good job of it as – wow! she was in her most cattish mood last night and streaked my hand with blood. She's quite a murderess in her ways and I should say has a sadistic streak in her nature.

Where does all this go – oh yes – the weather – isn't it fine – can you see in front of your nose. I cannot. We've been earth bound for some days now. Our last trip was to Hamburg but heavens knows where we landed. *Twas a dreadful night. I found myself over or very near Amsterdam on return – and nearly collapsed – wouldn't believe it – did I sweat the W/Op and my box – I'll say. I got about 12 fixes in as many minutes and even then was inclined to believe Jerry was faking them. However a belt of searchlights convinced me that something must be the matter – so down went our nose – up went our speed and over the sea we roared at a rate of revs. I'm still trying to puzzle out what happened. Group went into a flat spin as all the planes went well and truly South on return and wondered what Jerry was up to – if he had jammed our gear or what not. Personally I think we were caught up into a hellish front and were driven south by it.*

Somehow I think Hamburg was fairly safe that night. When we landed on E.T.A.[1] at the target it was 10/10 cloud. Plenty of flak and broken patches of heavy stuff and lots of smokeless stuff hanging like huge balloons all round. We descended to 8000 ft. and still were in cloud, – so we had to drop our load on E.T.A. and set off home. However I don't suppose we can always have good visibility and A.1 conditions – but I don't like dropping bombs on E.T.A. and hoping for the best. Still I might get a lucky one in. We had to do the same the first time we went to Dusseldorf, and wow, that was the best raid on the town. The luck of the devil, I guess.

Here we are earth bound. I wonder if we'll get airborne tonight. Tis dreadful y'know – we have lectures each morning and P.T. in the afternoon. Wow – P.T. I'm hardly fit to walk these last two days after all this tugging and running. Queer game. Still we get a spot of fun out of it and it'll help the avoirdupois[2] down, and I believe I've gone up a pound or two.

Glad that you're having such a wizard time Infant and also that you are looking after yourself. I don't know when our leave will come round. I believe either the 1st or the 8th of next month. What a time since I last saw you. Still I guess you'll welcome the rest. Glad that you

---

[1] Estimated time of arrival

[2] Weight—thought he was becoming too plump

have finished up your typing. Will give you a little more time to your-self.

Cheerio dearest. Look after yourself and I do want to see you y'know, but circumstances do seem against it till the leave period comes round, still that's a fortnight or more ahead so one never knows.

All my love dearest,

Yours, Roo

Camp, Wednesday morn.

My Dear Belovedest,

Oh darling how I wish I hadn't been so stupid – I want you so much sweetheart. Darling, I love you, love you – that's all I want to say, all that is necessary to say – I do dear heart, I can't say how thankful I am dearest that you came to the station on Monday. We did have a mar-vellous few hours didn't we? The only hours that I've really enjoyed since the last time we were together – and dearest – that's true – Dar-ling I was ever so sorry to have to leave you in the middle of the way back to your bus. I asked at the picket post whether there was one to come and they said yes – so I was reassured that you had one to catch – I'd have come down if there hadn't been and risked the getting back.

We were on last night – phew I'm glad we didn't get off the deck. The Bomb Armourers couldn't get the bomb unit changed in time to get us off. We were going to <u>Kiel</u> and our 4000 lb. bomb was fitted up when he discovered the unit u/s[1] – with the possibility of it dropping off when the engines started. We were all of us jolly fagged and it would have meant plenty of caffeine – we weren't sorry really – tho' the trip would have been pretty good I think. All of the kites got back O.K. so that speaks volumes. They're all in bed now so we haven't heard any details. I went to bed at 8 o'clock and never woke till 8.30 this morn-ing – just in time to get breakfast. Devine was as I was aussi and

---

[1] Unserviceable

between the two of us we left the wireless and the light on all night and slept through it. He is 21 today – and feeling jolly pleased with himself.

Tweedles J.C. is in the best of health and was she glad to see us. Her maidenly modesty forbids her to sleep so close to me now – for I found her at the foot of my bed this morning – so I presume that she had been there all night.

Darling heart I want this to get the post at 10 o'clock so forgive me for it being so short. I hope you got the one I sent you from Grantham. Darling I'm coming to see you the first time I can get away for a few hours from this place. So if I suddenly send a telegram or a 'phone message you'd understand won't you. Darling I love you sincerely and its you, just you sweetheart mine. Cheerioh darling, Thank God you're you.

All my love, dear heart,

Yours, Roo

Darling you're sweet – I never realised how much your caresses meant till you were in my arms darling. It was heaven – and I'm not sloppy really you know. It was and it is.

Same Place, Friday

Dearest Rabbit,

Whatever is the matter dearest no letter since Tuesday. However here goes – if the mountain won't come to Mahomet – then Mahomet will have to visit the mountain. Not much news of any kind to tell you except I've had the miserable misfortune to be on another funeral parade – Why on earth do they pick on me – I'll have to get a mirror and see if I perchance resemble an undertaker and it'll be an idea perhaps for apres la guerre fini poor old ?Mattans? – our 41 CO. O. Chop.[1]

Bad show really – still – that's how it goes. Now for pleasanter topics. Ain't the weather just wonderful. Hell's Bells we've been grounded for at least a fortnight now – of course we are always flying – always making out trips – but never flying them. Still a wind decided to raise itself from its sleep last night and howled round the hut making a helluva din – so it might shift the Cold Front along a bit and let us get cracking again. Good news from the Egyptian Front what. I wonder how long we can keep them on the move – forever I hope – then perhaps we can get moving on an offensive here – It seems a long cry since Milan but I don't believe we've actually flown more than 10 hrs. since then and I doubt if any of them have been ops. Can't remember much – Been busy on a couple of jobs fooling around in the Bombing Section.

Don't know if and when my course will come off. Poor old West[2] *nearly gave birth to an idea when he heard that perhaps I'd be away for 2 weeks. His faith in me is pathetic really – Still he'll learn the hard way what it is to have a lazy navigator. I may even get busy on a spot of Astro soon if we haven't forgotten how to use the Astro-graph. Well well, enough of shop. I'm sick of shop really.*

What have you been doing lately? Hitting the high spots? Have your good times dearest but don't be silly and get yourself ill again. Quite easy to do y'know. As for me I've been too interested in the fire and the bunk to move far from it. Haven't been off the Camp since the last time I saw you. In fact I've developed into quite a stay at home. Guess I'll have to break out soon – 'tho where to I don't know. Buses are a problem I believe – but its too darn cold to venture far – and from here there's only Boston available as no buses run anywhere else at the time we're clear. S'awful but there 'tis.

Well darling before I drive you to sleep with my drivel – Cheerioh.

---

[1] Chop=killed.

[2] West was the pilot.

All my love dearest,

Yours Roo

P.S. You're still Tops

Same Place, Sunday

Dearest One,

How'st sweet? I hope the cold and all its attendant ills are vanquished forever from the realm of your majesty. Mine is in the stages of leaving me with a running nose (er, have you ever seen a nose running – I have visions of noses with small legs and arms – long nose – short nose – broad nose – small noses – hooked noses, straight noses, aye, even Grecian noses all roaring along the pavement doing sneezing exercises to the tune of Blow Bugle Blow by Ivor Cold.)

Have had two bad days – Friday and Sat. stayed in bed yesterday laid low by the M.O. – he caught up with my inoculation. The arm was O.K. but the head and the tummy – nuff said. Did I moan – however feel very much better today – ready for an ops. trip which was cancelled. Would have been a jolly good one too – Got at least 9 hrs. for it. We spent from 2 – 4.40 preparing our charts as we had alternative routes given us and when we had all finished – cancelled. Were we mad? Oh no! Such lovely weather we're having here too. Grey skies and rain – Does it ever do anything else but rain in this place – Is it as cold at C. as it is here! Wow! We've a fire in our billet all day – and have made surreptitious visits to the coal compound to pinch the black nuggets from beneath the wire – What a life. What a moan – When I think of that 2½ hrs. work this afternoon. I hope we do the trip tomorrow then we won't have to remake our plans. I'm getting pretty lazy in my old age, really am y'know.

I'm sorry about the day off dearest, but not possible I guess. We're here till our next leave is due. When that is I don't know – In about a month's time I think, but we may be able to get a 48 in between.

Trouble is we've had so many trips scrubbed[1] lately. 5 in a row – and – in fact we haven't flown since Milan. Terrible I calls it – really do – but there 'tis. Guess I'm doomed to this place for at least 18 months. I'm hoping that my Bombing Leaders' Course will come through in a fortnights time – but even that is dependent on a deal of a no. of factors.

Enough of this. Do you know sweet I really rather miss a certain young lady by the name of Sylvia – Tell her when you see her that I do will you. Wish I had had you with me to help the old head – er – y'know kind of Peter and Paul resting place. Sure it would have done the trick and soothed the fevered brow what!

Well dearest there's nothing more to tell you and I've gone through the list of moans. Getting quite good at that – so I guess before I bore you too much with vain repetition that the Gentiles use – I'd better draw this to a close. Hope you're having a good time – but are taking special care of yourself.

Cheerio for now dearest,

All my love,

Yours Roo

Same Place, Tuesday '42

Dearest One,

Was so pleased to get your letter today and to see that you are having such a good time. Glad the cold is O.K. Have been doing nothing much lately except to prepare trips and then have the work scrubbed. Good for the paper salvage I guess. Today we went on Manoeuvres to Wigsley and had to capture the drome – Help – what a deuce of a day. I'm in the process of thawing and drying out now. It rained a steady drizzle all the time – Had some fun clambering in and out ditches.

---

[1] cancelled

Managed to capture a gun post – and then had an all in go for it – some game what! Glad I'm not ground defence. I'd hate to have to go crawling along hedges and in ditches again. However I'll sleep well tonight – guess this will have to be a short note dear as I've got to go to Coningsby immediately – what for I don't know – What a life – no sooner back than off again – Have been doing a spot of reading lately – good for the brain box – mine has been pretty rusty of late so good to get the wheels greased again – Don't know when I'll be able to make it to see you – as it may be at – or rather will be at a minute's notice – if it ever does materialise – still we never knows ones prospects in this place. I had thought that as it was a stand down for us today, that we'd have the day off – but <u>NO</u>, so you see that's how it is – Tough isn't it – but it's a matter of becoming reconciled.

Thank your mother for her kind words – will write when can get myself down to it – I'm trying to catch up on back mail – but so far haven't succeeded much – still one drop of water helps to fill the bucket –

Cheerio for now dearest,

All my love

Yours Roo

❖ ❖ ❖

<u>LETTER CARD</u> *to LACW Pickering, S. J.*
c/o W.A.A.F. Guard Room, R.A.F. Camp, Cottesmore, Rutland

Same Place, Wednesday 9th[1]

Dearest,

Thanks for your note received on return – Unfortunately we were on last night and I had no opportunity of replying to same. Had quite a good trip – 11 hrs. 5 mts. and a V/G from the A.O.C. – really a piece of luck really as we managed to get a pin point for a run in just as we

---

[1] Letter probably written December 1942.

were about to give up the ghost – We were diverted to Great Mass-
ingham and couldn't get home for two days. We were on again on
Mannheim – but it was a lousy night and not as good a trip. Had 2
F.W. 190s on our tail for quite a time but lost them in cloud thank
goodness. Were on again last night but couldn't get off the deck – on
again tonight – Glad you're having a good time. Cheerioh for now.
God bless. Remember me to your mother.

Roo

❖ ❖ ❖

Camp, Monday.

Beloved One,

Was so nice to get your long letter yesterday, 'tho when I read how you
were dearest – well you know how I feel about you and your colds –
and I feel deucedly responsible for this one really and wish I were
there to give you the blue shoulder[1] – 'tho at the present moment we'd
only sniff and snuffle in unison and cough in discord – Darling you
don't take enough care of y'self y'know. Now, I know what you are
going to say – but let's look at it in this light – you feel slightly better
and (quite naturally) want to go out now that's where we've always
made the mistake – Dearest can't you ever get into your head that the
worst period of a cold is just about when it's just about to mend – and
then you need that extra rest to build up the old system and the resis-
tance – I can't help feeling you've been plugging yourself too hard – oh
I know its wanting to take yourself out of yourself – God knows I
know what that means still you've got to realise sweetheart that
you're not a "he-man" type and you just cannot – Well darling I guess
you've got to face the fact that you've got to take care of yourself – ex-
tra care sweetheart. Enough – I trust however that you are feeling
much better today – but do take care of yourself and <u>REST</u> – R E S T – I
know how dreadful that is but – then all –

---

[1] I used to say how I loved the dark blue of the Aussie uniform to snuggle into
when feeling depressed.

Now to get on to the other subject. Can I – I guess I can do almost any-thing – 'tis only a matter of perspective – I can even write love letters – funny that – I've even managed to write one – and if you keep your tongue in your cheek 'tis marvellous what you can do – so you ask me to live in the present, well the present contains you – so what? Isn't it you that's important – so I guess I can, but don't be surprised if I break down sometimes – after all I'm not a machine – but still I guess I can – but I warn you darling – the present to the present – and I guess you know we can have a present – Phew, what a jumble, can you make sense of it – my head is buzzing around a bit – so blame it on the head. These colds do catch you on the hop don't they – I've been grounded tonight and tomorrow – ear trouble the M.O. feared might develop and so I've been ordered to bed. I should be O.K. by Wednesday, so I hope will be flying then – all well and good.

Cheerioh for now dearest – sorry if I've been disjointed. Guess we'll take the present and make it <u>OURS</u>. Can <u>YOU</u> do that?

All my love, darling,

Yours, Roo

P.S. I <u>DO</u> hope you are feeling better dearest.

P.P.S. When do we see each other again?

10. *Diary – Autumn 1942*

No entries between 9th February 1941 and 30th September, 1942.

Wed. 30 Sept 1942	Dance Oakham. Met small W/Op/AG[1] "Red". Quite an enjoyable evening after all. No difference between English and Canadian ideas?
Thur. 1 Oct 1942	Duty Guard Room LACW[2] 2 new arrivals S.P.T. & M.T.[3] Got telephone exchange to wake me at 11.30. Dozed. Very tired when 'phone woke me up to go off duty.
Fri. 2 Oct 1942	After much persuasion by Mary Wood went to Dance. Had a WIZARD evening, met Mex Dent W/Op/A.G., charming, very interesting - came back with him.
Sat. 3 Oct 1942	To Grantham via Duty Lorry. Home 12 p.m. Rode "Sandy" at Sturton Show Musical Chairs - shirt tails came out. Back 5.50. Tiring day - cold made worse.
Sun. 4 Oct 1942	To first of series of Whist Drives in old W.A.A.F. Mess. Entrance money (6d.) for prize money. Four W.A.A.F. 82 men. Poor cards. 24 hands. Finis 10.45
Mon. 5 Oct 1942	Early to bed – did I need it - oh boy! Cold none too good – dosed myself with quinine. Benzedrine inhalers jolly good stuff.
Tues. 6 Oct 1942	Dancing class awful 'til 8.20 met W/Op/A.G. Jack Smith (554) - was in Saltby crash – broke back. Persuaded to stay until 10.30 missed bus - caught 11.45. To meet at W.V.S. tomorrow night – lent me his scarf - cold.
Wed. 7 Oct 1942	Expected to enjoy myself Oakham Dance. Awful show, Mex ignored me - Jack did not turn up. What do I do with J's scarf. Men sure are queer creatures. Shall I give them up? – P'raps.
Thurs. 8	ROO gone to London for leave - have hurt his feelings, thinks I don't

[1] Wireless Operator/Air Gunner

[2] Leading Aircraftwoman

[3] Sparking Plug Tester and Motor Transport

Oct 1942	want to see him. Mess up. Domestic Evening - plenty of darning to do!
Fri. 9 Oct 1942	Sewed new wings on greatcoat etc. ready to go with 'Awa to Thrapston to see his Aunts – told me in evening cancelled as they had colds. Back early - hair curling etc.
Sat. 10 Oct 1942	With 'Awa to Leicester for day. Lunch Lewis's. Long talk till 3 p.m. Shop gazing, tea, Odeon saw "Joan of Paris". Back 9.15. Wizard film, wizard day.
Sun. 11 Oct 1942	S/L not in a.m. Work O.K. - did stamps – Pitcairn Islands etc. dancing class till 8 - up with Mary Wood to Y.M.C.A. for choc. Then Whist Drive - 20 hands = 127.
Mon. 12 Oct 1942	Telegram from ROO - met him off 5 p.m. bus. Tea at canteen. Lots of talk, things much happier all round. Retnd G. 11.30 bus.
Tues. 13 Oct 1942	Back early, bath and bed 8.45. Felt needed some shut-eye; slept very solidly.
Wed. 14 Oct. 1942	Met 'Awa, on duty tonight. Wants me to go to flicks tomorrow - can't Domestic Evening. Meet at Kettering week on Sunday when he returns from leave. He certainly is sweet. S/Ldr not in all day. Not much work. Quite good dance, met "Bahamas" again. Blowers most attentive, took me to bus!!!
Thurs. 15 Oct 1942	D Evening. Lecture by Leicester professor "Courses after War" - pep talk quite good. In bed and asleep by nine p.m. Slept soundly.
Fri. 16 Oct 1942	V.V. cheesed. At lunch Blowers phoned!!! Persuaded to go to Dance. Wizard time; sherry at "George". B. can be charming when tries. How long will it last?!!!
Sat. 17 Oct 1942	Telegram from ROO. Met him at office 4.30. Oakham for tea. Cable from Ellie. How I wish I knew what to do for best. Why oh why has it to be so?
Sun. 18 Oct. 1942	Home 3 p.m. bus. Bus dep. Grantham 5.30. Tried to hitch via Sleaford. Nearly got stranded Lincoln 7.10. Bus did not leave until 8 p.m. 5½ hours to travel 50 miles.
Mon. 19 Oct 1942	Up 10.45. Picked almonds. Over ate on pork sausage meat - made absolute pig of myself. ROO met 5.50 bus. Tried to say I never would. Does hurt. No good for martyr!!
Tues. 20 Oct 1942	Am really too tired to enjoy myself properly. Must make myself have some early nights. Early to bed.
Wed. 21 Oct 1942	Early to bed again.
Thurs. 22 Oct 1942	Domestic Evening - back once again. AM looking forward to going out again to Dance at Oakham tomorrow. Hope cold keeps off.

Fri. 23 Oct 1942	Got everything ready to go to Dance - "best blues" etc. Cold steadily worse all day. Feel rotten. Everyone in Room giving me aspirins etc!
Sat. 24 Oct 1942	Cold bad - temp. 98.8° a.m. Half day in bed - S/L Johnson's orders. Feeling pretty sorry for myself! P.M. temp. normal
Sun. 25 Oct 1942	½ day in bed – temp. O.K. Gee, how I am longing to go out again.
Mon. 26 Oct 1942	Cold lots better. Decided to be on safe side - so to bed early AGAIN. It will be WIZARD to go out again - whoopee!!
Tues. 27 Oct 1942	Got 'Awa to take me to see "Moonlight over Burma" (not love story!) Brilliant moonlight night - 'AWA seemed affected by it. Not always definitely uncousinly.
Wed. 28 Oct 1942	To Dancing Class. Met B.L.H.V. Cadet L.E. Turner – Leo. Sweet kid - only 19.[1] Worked hard together at dancing class.
Thu. 29 Oct 1942	Once again Domestic Evening. Oh boy, do I appreciate going out now after having been in for so long or do I?!
Fri. 30 Oct 1942	Duty LACW in Guard Room – what a waste of a good evening when BRUSH wanted me to go to a dance, 'AWA to flicks and LEO to dance.
Sat. 31 Oct 1942	Met BRUSH 6.30 W.V.S. corner canteen and then to Dance. I am really getting quite fond of him.
Sun. 1 Nov 1942	Dancing Class. BRUSH came in before going to Sgts' Mess Dance on Camp (R.A.F. North Luffenham). Must learn to Tango - it's wizard.
Mon. 2 Nov 1942	To flicks with BRUSH - had not got bad hangover after all!! Long talk afterwards - most helpful.
Tue. 3 Nov 1942	Early to bed after hairdresser at 4.15. Drier u/s[2] so no setting lotion used - awful mess. 'AWA wants me to go to Kettering tomorrow to see his aunts. Promised to meet BRUSH.
Wed. 4 Nov 1942	8 a.m. start to Kettering to see Aunts B. & K. V. foggy. Late at Dance to meet BRUSH – had returned to Nth Luffenham to party. Feel a terrible pig for letting him down. Telephone girl would not give me his number
Thu. 5 Nov 1942	Domestic Evening yet once again. To bed early. Wonder how cross BRUSH will be about Wed?[3]

---

[1] I was just 20.

[2] Unserviceable

[3] He cycled 8 or 10 miles from North Luffenham to Oakham for Dance at which I arrived late due to being out for the day with my cousin from New Zealand

Fri. 6 Nov 1942	Dance with BRUSH. Learnt about Phyllis (his fiancée). Felt depressed - wish wasn't so terribly possessive, it is ridiculous. O.K. about Wed.
Sat. 7 Nov 1942	Dancing class of BRUSH's at N. L.[1] every Saturday – so back early. Bad cold seems to have taken a lot out of me.
Sun. 8 Nov 1942	D. Class – met blonde S/Pilot Grove. V. charming. Persuaded him to go to Whist Drive. Marvellous manners – although English!
Mon. 9 Nov 1942	"Caught in the Draft" with BRUSH. Entertaining but rest boring - tired – went to sleep. Found cider! Scared B. by piece of acting – unfortunate. Didn't know I was such a good actress.
Tues. 10 Nov 1942	BRUSH 'phoned to see if I was O.K. Most anxious. Promised to go to bed early. In by 8.5!! Asleep 8.25!!
Wed. 11 Nov 1942	D. Class. S. GROVE must have seen me when sat 3 rows behind B. and me in flicks. Nothing doing at all! Bad show. Met "ROLY" – Canadian Lac - quite nice.
Thur. 12 Nov 1942	D. Evening. W/CDR GARDNER gave talk on Training Wing. Too terribly boring as I work in T.W. myself.
Fri. 13 Nov 1942	To Dance with BRUSH. BRUSH forgave my acting which I did last time I saw him. Am glad.
Sat. 14 Nov 1942	Enjoyed Dance so much last night that we went again tonight, but being Sat. too crowded and left early.
Sun. 15 Nov. 1942	Church bells[2] rang for first time since June '40. Volunteered for Church Parade in Station Workshop Church. 1st time I had been in there. Early to bed.
Mon. 16 Nov 1942	To flicks with BRUSH, saw "Moonlight over Burma" I think but can't really remember. BRUSH goes on 7 days leave tomorrow.
Tues. 17 Nov 1942	Couldn't leave Camp until 1600. Leo biked with me to Gt. North Road and took bike back for me. Hitched in Commando lorry to Grantham. Reached Ivy's. Joy[3] there. Pigeon pie supper. Talked with Joy 1 a.m. Slept on couch.
Wed. 18 Nov 1942	Slept till woken 11.50. Saw rabbits. Roast chicken dinner. Bridget pleased to see me, had WIZARD ride with Joy and Ivy over jumps on top farm. Jumped perfectly. Returned to Camp.

[1] North Luffenham

[2] Church bells were allowed to be rung to celebrate the victory at El Alamein a railway junction on the coast road of northern Egypt. It gave its name to a decisive battle (1942) of World War II when the 8th Army defeated Rommel's Afrika Corps.

[3] Her daughter

Thu. 19 Nov 1942	D. Evening. To sleep early. Mummy going down to Gosport this week-end. Still having treatment at St. Thomas'.[1]
Fri. 20 Nov 1942	'AWA told me of possible engagement to Kay Wiggins. (Quick work!!) Wonder what will come of it. To Dance with 'AWA – Quite nice time.
Sat. 21 Nov 1942	Hockey v. Melton Mowbray Old Grammarians away. U/S'd toe. Nice tea - but not enough of it! Transport returned early – back at Exton 7 p.m.
Sun. 22 Nov. 1942	All morning waiting for M.O. who only pinched toe and said come again tomorrow! S/Ldr gave me p.m. off. Sat in Y.M.C.A. Wrote to Tubby.
Mon. 23 Nov 1942	Leo posted to Brighton yesterday. Sorry did not see him. Spent all this morning waiting to see M. O. again. Back early – laundering.
Tue. 24 Nov. 1942	In lorry 12 a.m. to Rauceby[2] for X-ray to toe. Bone cracked – O.K. to Dance when feel like it. Kept everyone waiting. Camp 8 p.m. Toe a lot better.
Wed. 25 Nov 1942	BRUSH returned leave last night. To flicks - "Mercy Island". Forest ranger badge? Enjoyable evening.
Thu. 26 Nov 1942	Domestic Evening. ROO arrived. 1st time seen him for 6 weeks. Strained atmosphere, even Mary could feel it. To Leic by 8 a.m. transport tomorrow.
Fri. 27 Nov 1942	Shopping Leicester with ROO. V. foggy. p.m. Flicks "Ten Gentlemen from West Point". Returned 6.15 train. Cpl Bullot returned with us – luckily. Flicks Oakham "Hold that Ghost" – funny.
Sat. 28 Nov 1942	S/L gave (me) p.m. off. To Melton Mowbray with ROO 3.30 bus. Tea "Anne of Cleeves" cafe. Flicks "Maltese Falcon". Retnd 10 p.m. bus. ROO feeling V cut up - thinks (I) have "played him for a sucker".
Sun. 29 Nov. 1942	Saw ROO at lunch – went to London p.m. Am amazed how callous I feel towards him. GREAT relief everything is over. However could I feel like I did?
Mon. 30 Nov 1942	1st Dance since toe u/s with BRUSH, Mary (Wood) and Les Hollins.[3] Celebrated Les's crowns.[4] Lovely time but missed Tango. Back 11.30 bus – dangerously late.[1]

---

[1] St. Thomas's Hospital in London

[2] R.A.F. Hospital

[3] Mary's Link Trainer Instructor friend

[4] When promoted to Flight Sergeant from Sergeant a "gold" crown is worn above the sergeants stripes.

Tues. 1 Dec. 1942	Oakham 5.12. Shopping, tea. "Model Wife" with BRUSH. 10.30 transport. Thought of Phyllis does not bother me at all now. BRUSH is a good pal - tore me off a strip last night for getting in a temper! Shook me horribly!
Wed. 2 Dec 1942	Dance 7 p.m. Went by myself – mostly boring - 'tho O.K. towards the end. Bdr during dance W/OP/AG coming back. V. cold, first really frosty night.
Thu. 3 Dec 1942	Dom Eve. Lecture – Major Casey - "Station Defence". Asleep 8.45. V. tired. BRUSH 'phoned 1330 – Couldn't go to Dance last night owing to C.O's inspection.

NOTE: I have enjoyed re-reading these entries after a gap of 55 years – they were written in a blue "Five Year Diary" which had a little lock on it to keep my memories secure!

SGT. "Brush" BLOWERS

Brush is mentioned in the Diary from Wed. 14 Oct. 42 onwards. He was a Link Trainer Instructor at R.A.F. North Luffenham, who also taught ballroom dancing one night a week at the Camp. He acquired his nickname because of his strong head of hair, which usually stood up like a shaving brush.

We met at the Victoria Dance Hall in Oakham and became good friends and dancing partners. Under his excellent tuition I lost my nervous ramrod stiffness and became both relaxed and proficient. My favourite was the tango to the tune of "Jealousy". In one of his letters Roo said "Glad you are improving in your dancing ... still you have a competent teacher".

At Christmas the WAAF at Exton Hall were permitted to gather greenery from the grounds to decorate the splendid front hall which had a super parquet floor and fine well pol-

---

[1] Must be in by 2359 hrs!

ished carved furniture, and to hold a small dance there for our friends. Brush cycled all the way from North Luffenham to partner me on that festive occasion.

MY NEW ZEALAND COUSIN

Below is a photo of my distant New Zealand cousin, taken in November 1942, just before gaining his Commission in the Royal Air Force as an Observer (Navigator). We met at Cottesmore for the first time when I was stationed there and he was nearly at the end of his training on either Hampden or Wellington bombers.

'Awa (as I called him) came home on leave with me and I went with him to visit his aged Aunts in Kettering. I thought he was gorgeous – tall, dark, handsome and fell for him hook, line and sinker! When I had to go around Camp taking files to various Sections, many were the lengthy detours I made in the hope of seeing him. When girls quizzed me saying "Who was that good looking chap you were out with last night who was wearing N.Z. shoulder flashes?"

I replied "My cousin."

"A likely story," they retorted.

It was not long before 'Awa became engaged to a very smart WAAF who worked in the Equipment Section.

Kay Wiggins wore a well tailored uniform of "officer type" material, bought privately. She was always impeccably turned out and appeared full of confidence. I was very envious.

11. *A sad parting*

It was too good to last. I had had almost two very happy years as Clerk G.D. to the Armament Officer F/Lt Johnson, sharing an office with him in the centre of the Camp behind Station Sick Quarters. Then when he was promoted S/Ldr Armament he took me with him to a huge hangar at the edge of the airfield where he had his own quite pleasant office and mine was a rather draughty place at the edge of the hangar and my friendly Armoury companions were back at the Armoury some distance away.

For me to be happy in my work I must both like and respect my boss. For I cannot (or will not) disguise my true feelings about anyone – which is often most unfortunate, as you will find out if you continue to read this!

I would sometimes say to my super South African boss that I did not think that something or other was fair or that I thought it ought to be done differently. F/Lt Johnson would always say: "What have YOU done to change things for the better?" Because I thought so highly of him, this attitude to things which I thought were wrong, I subsequently tried to change, which led me to confrontation with my Senior Medical Officer boss on posting to R.A.F. Coningsby.

After Christmas in 1942 I was told that I was to go home on Compassionate Leave to nurse my mother who was ill. I knew that we periodically used to go up to London together for my mother to visit St. Thomas's Hospital for treatment but I had not fully appreciated the significance of it all. Our Doctor had wanted me to come home before Christmas to nurse her, but she had refused to make the request for this, as she wanted me to have a happy Christmas on Camp with all my friends, rather than being at home nursing her, with only my elderly Father for company other than herself.

My Mother – Elizabeth Cathleen Holtom (Betty)

I was issued with a railway warrant but I did not use it as it was quicker to hitch hike along the Great North Road to Grantham and then on to Lincoln and by bus to Saxilby.

Shortly after my return home Dr. Maiden, our very nice local G.P. came to see my mother. After seeing her we walked down the driveway from our home together in the winter's cold and utter pitch darkness of the blacked-out village. I asked Dr. Maiden "How long will it be with my Mother?" Meaning, how long before she returns to better health. Dr. Maiden did not realise that I did not know my mother was dying. He replied that in cases like this it was impossible to tell – she might live for days, several weeks or a month or two. We parted without further conversation and he never knew what a shock his words had been to me. I wrote to Harold and told him of the situation and this was his reply:

Officers Mess, Cottesmore

Tuesday

Hello Bunty,

Thank you for the letter my Dear, sorry to hear your Mother has taken a turn for the worse. I do hope that it is only a passing result of what she has been through.

I know how you feel Bunty, and do admire you for the brave way you are facing up to things. I wish I could be with you all the time to help share some of your burden. Yes, I too thought your Dad seemed a bit unconcerned. Does he know how serious things are, maybe he doesn't realize or does but is one of those who doesn't show their feelings.

I took your note or at least the Doctors note into the Orderly Room as Mrs ? wasn't in, the Flt/Sgt said it was quite alright. Have you heard anything from Group about your temporary release?

Kay came over to Leicester on Saturday night and stayed til Sunday. I went over and we both went along to see the Rev. Davies, I guess we will be taking the plunge sometime in March, the latter part of March.

I think if things turn out in the way we sincerely hope they won't, you had better come out to New Zealand, that is of course if you don't go on overseas service. Come over afterwards in any case. Well, my Dear, there is not much I can say except keep a brave heart, put your trust in the only One.

Give your dear Mother my earnest love and wish her a speedy return to good health. Chin up.

Your cousin and friend always,

Harold

(Until leaving for Boarding School in 1936 I was always known as Bunty – and am still known by that name by many people.)

My mother and I used to speak of her forthcoming death as "preparing for a journey" as it was so hard for us to make these unhappy plans when we were so close to each other and if we were not very careful, we both ended up in tears. I was her only child. My father, twenty years her senior, had had four daughters by his first wife who had died. These daughters were more or less the same age as my mother. In fact, my mother met my father through one of his daughters. My mother was governess to the two children at the nearby Manse when Ivy, father's eldest daughter, was at Art Class in Lincoln at the Technical College and my mother was there too. My mother was invited to "Moorlands" to play tennis and there met my widowed father – in due course, I became the result of that meeting. I think he was disappointed that with a "new" wife he had yet another daughter – me.

One afternoon I came back from the village and went quietly into my mother's room and found she appeared to be sleeping with her mouth and eyes partly open. I had never encountered death before but I felt sure that this must be it. Nevertheless, having read in stories about using a mirror at the lips to detect breathing, I did just that. This confirmed my belief that my beloved mother was free of pain at last and had started on her journey for which we had been making earthly plans.

We had arranged a traditional funeral for her at the village Church a short distance away to which she was to be taken in a horse drawn hearse which would have to come out from Lincoln six miles away. I remember the carriage in which I travelled as a very ancient vehicle that smelt dusty and un-cared for, as we rocked slowly towards the Church with the black plumes on the horses' bridles gently nodding.

My mind is a blank after we got to the Church. I remember my surprise and pleasure to find that my Aussie friend, Roo, had not been on ops. so was able to come over and support me at this, the unhappiest time of my short life. He knew my parents and had an open invitation to stay at "White Lodge" whenever he wanted a break from ops. – he was a Navigator on Lancaster bombers at the time. We had met at 14 O.T.U. Cottesmore in 1941 when I was Clerk to the Station Armament Officer and Roo finished his O.T.U. training there – probably on Hampdens as I don't think Wellingtons were there until after his posting to an operational squadron. So, Roo was a trusted friend whom I had known for over a year. A long time in those days.

On one occasion I had been sent home from R.A.F. Cottesmore Sick Bay before I was well enough to travel which resulted in my being away from duty for five weeks and nearly delirious in bed with a very high temperature and pulse rate. My mother allowed Roo to sit by my bed looking after me. In Oz Roo was a teacher, married with a son. He told me he was unhappily married and intended to go on ops. until he did not return, as he would not go back to Australia alive. So, right from the start, I knew that he was "forbidden territory" and I must not get too fond of him. We used to spend a lot of time in a little Church Army Canteen in nearby Oakham when we were at R.A.F. Cottesmore and I can always remember the dear motherly ladies behind the counter there asking when we were going to become engaged, as they thought we looked right for each other and very happy together. I don't remember what I said but we did not break their romantic illusions by saying that I was going out with a married man. This was NOT done in the 1940's.

Later, when Roo started operational flying from R.A.F. Woodhall Spa with 97 Squadron we used to try and meet in Lincoln whenever possible. He often brought with him, from his flying rations, lovely little tins of condensed orange juice or some Horlicks tablets. These were most welcome as I believe our sweet ration was 3ozs per week – if the NAAFI had any stocks.

So, to return to the graveside of my mother. Immediately the Service was over Roo and I left for a long walk together. I don't remember anything about the mourners or what arrangements were made for the reception afterwards. Everyone had been very shocked by what was, to them, my mother's unexpected death, as she hadn't wanted others to know that she was dying.

Roo was about eight years older than I in years but a great deal more in his knowledge of the world. After my mother's death I knew that I should want to lean on Roo a great deal more and that this must not happen – as he was married. So, on this walk I told Roo that we must not meet again until I was strong enough not to need to lean on him for comfort. That was the last time we met.

I do not know what happened after that cold day in February when my mother was buried and I said goodbye to Roo. From my letter to him on 11th March, 1943 I see I had been to stay with my Uncle at Gosport.

> *White Lodge,*
>
> *Saxilby, Lincoln*
>
> *11th March, 1943*
>
> *Dear Roo,*
>
> *Sorry I have not replied to your letter[1] before now, but I have been terribly busy.*
>
> *How's things with you? Have you nearly finished your ops. yet?*
>
> *Actually the above is not where I am at the moment, for I am having a spot of leave in Portsmouth, but am returning home on Tuesday.*
>
> *Went to Harold's wedding in Leicester on Monday. I quite enjoyed myself and "celebrated" so much that I nearly went to sleep in the train going to Town in the evening!*
>
> *Spent the night with Mrs. Grindell and had great fun shopping next morning with her.*
>
> *Excitement – bought a new hat. The first time I had bought anything new to wear for two years.*

---

[1] In the first paragraph of my letter I refer to a letter from Roo, which was still unanswered. As he never received this one from me dated March 1943, perhaps that is why I never heard from him again. The letter to Roo was postmarked GOSPORT, 12th March, 1943. 18th March 1943 postmarked Stromness, Orkneys, comment: "Not in Sgts' Mess Kinloss. 5th April 1943 postmarked Forres, Morayshire, comment: "Not called for, return to sender" also rubber stamped "UNDELIVERED FOR REASON STATED—RETURN TO SENDER"

Well if you will drop me a line to Saxilby stating you are still in the land of the living (cheerful aren't I?), I will drop you a longer line.

All the best,

Sylvia

My uncle was Surgeon Captain Holtom stationed, I believe, at the RN hospital Haslar and I had just been to my N.Z. cousin Harold's smart wedding near Leicester. (So why I bought a hat afterwards – I cannot imagine!) I was the only member of his family there as his two aged aunts in Kettering would not have been able to travel to the Wedding and everyone else was in New Zealand. He looked gorgeous in his officer's uniform. To him, I think I was just his "little kid cousin in England". He gave me a "Tikki" a New Zealand Maori charm to keep me safe and bring me luck but sadly it was later stolen with some other items when I was on my way home with all my kit after being demobbed and could not carry it all at once. His kindness was typical as was his most generous offer of a home in New Zealand if my mother died but I knew I could never take it up.

I know that sometime in the Spring of 1943, when I was feeling stronger, I wrote a long letter to Roo. It was returned to me marked, I believe, "missing – Return to sender". Somewhere amongst my possessions that unopened letter still lies. Over the years I have occasionally come across it – still unopened and unread since I wrote it whilst I was serving so unhappily at R.A.F. Coningsby.

As my Father, in his mid seventies, would now be living alone it was arranged that an officer and his wife from R.A.F. Scampton (about nine miles away) would share the house with him and see that all was well. My Father was a skilled and keen gardener and used to spend most of his time working in our large garden where we had big flower beds, two lawns and grew all our vegetables. He also used to like to go to Lincoln twice a week on market days so that he could meet his old farming friends, followed by card playing and chatting in his Club.

By then I was looking forward to returning to Camp and once again being amongst supportive friends after the stressful time I had had at home on compassionate leave nursing my dying mother. However, a nasty shock awaited me on my return. I found another WAAF had permanently taken over my job and that I had been posted away from all my friends and from a job I enjoyed to new strange surroundings at R.A.F. Coningsby.

There was nothing for it but to take the "Clearance Chit" around the Camp to get it signed and pack up all my gear and that of "Giddy Biddy" my mare. Fortunately my sister and her husband agreed to have Biddy temporarily on their farm at Leadenham, a village half way between Grantham and Lincoln. Biddy and I were both unfit and definitely tired by the time we had ridden just over 25 miles to our destination. Much of our journey was alongside the Great North Road (the A.1) but being wartime, with stringent petrol rationing, there was little traffic to bother us. These days the road is at least twice as wide as it was then and the huge wide grass verges have disappeared and the traffic is now probably one hundred fold.

12. *To RAF Coningsby*

On joining the WAAF I had been asked where I would like to be posted and had requested my home county of Lincolnshire. Admittedly Lincolnshire had so very many airfields in it, therefore, this probably did not offer great difficulties for those in charge of postings but at least "the powers that be" were kind to me and my three postings in the five years were always relatively suitable for home visits on "48" passes or longer Leaves.

I found that I had been posted to R.A.F. Coningsby, which was about 17 miles from Lincoln with a good rail service. (Now it is even difficult to find where the railway lines used to run – the whole track has been removed). My home village of Saxilby was only six miles the other side of Lincoln with a good hourly bus service.

Once I reported to R.A.F. Coningsby, a Lancaster Bomber Station, I was thankful to find that I had escaped being posted to the Orderly Room but was to be Clerk to the Senior Base Station Medical Officer and would be the only Clerk working in the Station Sick Quarters. As I was a fully trained Secretary Shorthand/Typist perhaps this is why I was given the job. I always feared the Orderly Room – at the beck and call of all and bossed by a fierce WAAF Sergeant – at least that is what I imagined – probably wrongly! As it so happens, I would probably have been much happier if that fate had befallen me.

I had no difficulties whatsoever with my duties. I was responsible for keeping in order medical files for all except officers on the Station – when necessary requesting files for people who were posted into the Camp or sending them off for those who were posted elsewhere. Typing out reports on patients who had been to see Specialists at R.A.F. Hospital Rauceby and attending to all the usual correspondence emanating from an R.A.F. Base Station Sick Quarters. I was also responsible for checking the files of everyone to ensure that their inoculations were up-to-date and arranging for inoculation sessions to be held at S.S.Q. when needed and then writing up their record cards appropriately afterwards. (I am ashamed to admit to being a coward about inoculations and "fiddled" them as needed on my own records).

I seem to remember that the S.S.Q was in a rather isolated position at the edge of the Camp near a one time public road and we operated as a self contained unit. Apart from the M.Os the rest of us had all our food sent over and we ate it in a room in S.S.Q. The Waafery was about a mile and a half away at the other side of the village and I used to cycle on my old Raleigh bicycle, with the cotter pin squeaking protestingly at every revolution of the wheel, to sleep in a Nissen hut when I was not on duty at S.S.Q. As I left in the morning in time to have breakfast at S.S.Q., followed by lunch and the early evening meal, I rarely met the other girls in the hut at the Waafery. When I was off duty I think I usually used to cycle to the railway station, leave my bike there, spend the evening in Lincoln, then pick up my bike on the return journey from Lincoln and cycle to the Waafery and so to bed.

Strangely I do not remember how many staff were employed at S.S.Q. I only remember some – the S/Ldr Senior Medical Officer and his two young F/O Medical Officers, an

R.A.F. Medical F/Sgt, a WAAF Medical Cpl, some Medical Orderlies and two WAAF Aircrafthands General Duties (ACH/GDs) one of which was a very good natured girl called Betty Doe.

As I was a Clerk G. D. my duties were normal office hours beginning when I had cycled in from the WAAF camp for my breakfast in S.S.Q., working there all morning, then the midday meal there followed by work in the afternoon and the early evening meal and then – OFF DUTY!

I found that the two unfortunate WAAF ACH.GD girls were on duty all day as normal and then had to sleep at S.S.Q. on alternate nights as well, as they did alternate nights on "Stand-By Duty". This merely meant being in Sick Quarters so that they were handy to do odd jobs at night in case of crashes or other emergencies – fill kettles, take messages etc. so they were on duty or on call for 36 hrs. at a stretch, had an evening and night off and then did another 36 hrs. on duty. In order to ease their long hours I offered to do a duty also and my offer was accepted. So then we each had a night on duty every third night instead of the two girls doing it alternate nights. It was never suggested to me that I should do any night duty at all.

We were quite a small group of people who ate and worked (and slept?) together day in and day out and I think this was probably what caused a lot of tensions amongst us. In those days of night duty waiting for an emergency to happen there was nothing to do, there was no television or video to watch, in fact, I don't even remember there being a radio there – we didn't even play cards. For example, the WAAF Cpl liked the F/Sgt so if he showed an interest in me the flames of jealousy were visible and I had to watch out that she could not fault me over anything! (I admit to being very careful when once I accepted his invitation to be shown round the Crash Room where aircrew were first taken for treatment when the Ambulance had brought them to S.S.Q.). I was permitted to try what it was like to lie on the Radiant Heat Bed. It really was amazing the wonderfully comforting warmth which emanated from the cover over one when lying on it. The arc of the cover over the bed ensured nothing touched the body to cause further pain to the crash victim. I could only imagine how desperately cold some of those crash victims must have been by the time they got back to this country in a damaged kite. In all probability they would have been wounded by the enemy or injured in the crash as well.

Three things stick in my memory from R.A.F. Coningsby. The Mortuary was fairly close to S.S.Q. On one occasion very badly burned bodies from a crash were in there. The strange sickly sweet stench, which crept across from these tragic victims to S.S.Q. is memorable to me even now, fifty years and more later.

Another tragedy, which I can still remember well, occurred over the Christmas festivities to a young aircrew officer at R.A.F. Woodhall Spa a few miles away. He was in bed after a very convivial party. During the night he felt very thirsty and reached out for the squash bottle near his bed thinking he would have a refreshing, long, cooling drink to assuage his thirst. Unfortunately his batman had used the old bottle for cleaning fluid ready to use on his officer's uniform and had left it within reach of his officer's bed on that fatal night. I well remember being told that the young officer had been rushed to Rauceby Hospital and his life was in grave danger due to the caustic effects of the cleaning fluid on his stomach. He fought for his life for several days but did not win.

My third vivid memory concerns a girl in my hut on the WAAF site where I used to sleep two nights out of three. I don't remember her name or even ever seeing her. It was probably winter time for, in the darkness of the hut she and her friends would discuss her wedding plans, for she had arranged to get married as soon as her fiancé had finished his tour. I remember the tension which gradually increased as he got closer and closer to the magic figure of 30 ops completed for then he would be assured of a good break from operational flying and his marriage would take place.

Although I never spoke to her myself, nevertheless I used to listen anxiously each night to find out how many more ops he still had to do. All was going well. Six – five – four – three – two… From then on there was no more talking in the darkness each night, only weeping in the bed at the far end of the hut.

Now, in lighter vein, a little story to show how naive I was; even after over two years in the WAAF I still thought all R.A.F. Medical Officers were heroes. We had two young MOs at Coningsby – one who was rather dashing and gorgeous and the other tall, dark and rather serious. One day I noticed an airman in the distance limping his way towards Sick Bay, obviously hoping for treatment. To my amazement the dashing, handsome young M.O. looked out and saw the airman also – then said "I'm going off duty now, before that man gets here!" I was shocked to think my dashing young God had feet of clay and was going to leave his more seriously minded colleague to treat the airman!

Whilst I was at Coningsby my appointment with the Eye Specialist at R.A.F. Hospital Rauceby came up. I have had an alternating squint since birth – and some embarrassing pictures of myself lying naked on a rug on the lawn wearing spectacles to prove it! It was hoped that the squint could be corrected.

I remember the Surgeon telling me that there "was nothing to it – you don't have to have a general anaesthetic – they just take your eye out on your cheek and do the job there". This news shocked rather than comforted me as I had had general anaesthetics before and much preferred to be oblivious to what was being done to me on such occasions. Nevertheless, I had always been embarrassed by my squint when I was not wearing glasses so agreed to the op going ahead. I found it just as frightening as I feared it would be. Both eyes were bandaged for several days afterwards.

It was about this time that I had my twenty-first birthday but I did not tell anyone about it. In those days of long ago, twenty-first birthdays were usually very special with lots of presents, a big party and extra privileges. On this occasion I was busy working late in my office and when I eventually got to the kitchen found that they had all had fried fish and in the big Mess tins all that was left were some congealing black fish skins from whence all flesh had been removed. Naturally enough no one had realised it was my birthday – let alone my 21st! There was not even one card from my father.

In fact the only occasion I remember having a letter from him was when I told him that I planned to go on leave with Ken and his crew to Edinburgh for a week. On receiving news of this projected holiday my father wrote to say that he did not expect a daughter of his to do such a thing. I wrote back to say that if he meant what I thought he meant – there was no need for me to go all the way up to Edinburgh in order to do it!

As a matter of fact Daddy knew and liked Ken, who was an Aussie M/U Gunner with 460 R.A.A.F. Squadron at R.A.F. Binbrook high up on the Lincolnshire Wolds north of Lincoln. Ken was welcome to stay at our home in Saxilby anytime he felt he needed a break from flying. Ken was very good at skinning a rabbit or plucking and gutting a chicken – I think these practical skills appealed to my father as a possible son-in-law. Ken was a most accomplished dancer and we had met in a Dance Hall in Lincoln and we used to meet in Lincoln whenever we were free to do so usually to dance together or occasionally "splashing out" on a 5/- dinner at the Grand Hotel or Albion (now The Barbican) near the Station.

The S/Ldr S. M. O. and I were constantly at loggerheads. I often thought he made some unfair decisions regarding his staff and that the staff were too much in awe of him except to grumble amongst themselves, so I was foolish enough to tackle him on their behalf and drew all his wrath onto my shoulders. In his office he had called me "a Disturbing Influence", "a Subversive Element" and "a Bolshie". I am not sure now whether all three epithets were used on the same occasion or on three separate summons to his sanctum. Needless to say I was NOT a happy WAAF. I asked around to see if my older and wiser Aussie friend Roo was still at R.A.F. Woodhall Spa a few miles away but he had disappeared – I did not know whether he was dead or alive. I am sure that if he and I had still been seeing each other, I should not have got myself into so much trouble as he would have calmed me down.

I saw on Daily Routine Orders that there was a need for WAAF to volunteer to go on a Cypher Course and, if successful, would be re-graded and posted overseas with the rank of Sgt. Years previously, when I belonged to the Girl Guides of Lincoln Girls' High School, a friend and I had travelled one Saturday to Lincoln on the bus for the Meeting and had missed the bus back to Saxilby from the Brayford. So rather than wait an hour for another one, for the only time in my life, I walked the six miles or so with her along the banks of the old Roman Fossdyke Canal and together we learnt the Morse Code on the journey. Thus emboldened I volunteered – anything to get away from Coningsby S.S.Q. Unfortunately I did not get even as far as the course. When my Medical records were examined it was seen that I had had an eye operation recently, which rendered me unsuitable. It was thought that the Cypher Sgts were going to Africa where the sand and dust would cause too many problems for my vision. So I could not even escape overseas!

I met the very nice S/Ldr Equipment Officer who said he would effect a swap so that I could go and work for him. Nothing happened. Maybe the S.M.O. would not let the exchange take place as he wished to "sort me out" himself. I don't know. He could not put me on a "Charge" because my work was always efficient. This impasse went on for what seemed to be ages and ages.

Eventually it was arranged that I should be posted to H.Q. 5 Group Bomber Command at R.A.F. Morton Hall, Swinderby near Lincoln in an exchange with a Clerk from Group H.Q.

With what joy I got "cleared" and left R.A.F. Coningsby with a glad heart! Whatever my future posting held in store I could not be more unhappy than I was at Coningsby.

NOTE: Three good things about Coningsby – it was always warm in S.S.Q., no queuing for meals – only time on parade was for pay fortnightly. I have been surprised to discover recently that I was only at Coningsby from March to November 1943 – it seemed very much longer than that.

Sketch map of Coningsby area (not to scale)

13. *Bridget goes to Coningsby*

I thought it might be difficult to find anywhere to keep my mare, Bridget, when I was posted to R.A.F. Coningsby in Lincolnshire. The village is situated on the edge of the very fertile flat fenlands which, particularly in wartime, were ploughed up and producing food on every available acre and there were very few grass fields where a horse could graze. Fortunately the River Bain ran close to the village on its journey to join the nearby River Witham and the land which bordered the river was grassland as, in winter time, it was often flooded and too wet for growing food crops.

I managed to find a small farmer who had some grazing at Tattershall Bridge and Biddy was installed in one of his riverside fields close to Coningsby village about one and a half miles from the WAAF Site which was on the opposite side of Coningsby village.

It was not a pleasant area in which to ride as there were no bridleways and the roads cut across the Fens in boring straight lines for mile after mile with not even a tree to break the monotony of the view. I needed smooth grass verges to ride on, as Bridget was not shod, therefore, the hard road surface soon wore her feet down too much, like a coarse nail file. So I rode only occasionally as there was too much hassle in getting ready for the ride and even when you were mounted at last, nowhere enjoyable to ride.

One of my childhood ambitions had been to breed a foal from my own mare, bring it up from birth myself and then train it so that I could ride it and bring forth any talent it might possess in any field – no pun intended!

I discovered that at Frithville, a wee village about seven miles away across the Fens towards Boston, there was a thoroughbred stallion named Burgundian whose father was The Recorder by the Derby winner Captain Cuttle. I thought that such an aristocratic fellow would make an ideal mate for Biddy who was about three-quarters thoroughbred. She was now middle aged and if she was going to be a mother it was about time she got started in the maternity stakes.

Punch accompanies Bridget and me out for a hack.

So on one of my days off we hacked along those boring Fen roads to see Burgundian and his owner, Mr. Thomas Balderson, at their little farm. When we got there I put Bridget temporarily in a stable and went to see the potential bridegroom. However, I never got a really good look at him except over the top of his stable door as he was very restive and went storming round his loose box, his chestnut coat glistening and looking every inch a very handsome beast – although he never stood still long enough for me to get a really good look at him.

As far as I knew Burgundian was the only potential mate for Biddy within reach of our being able to ride over to meet him – for I had no transport and petrol coupons would not have been available for such a wedding, even if I had had transport.

So, the marriage was arranged and when the date was considered suitable I rode over to Frithville for the marriage to be consummated. Unfortunately Biddy had other ideas and would have nothing to do with Burgundian, in fact, she threatened to kick his teeth in if she got half a chance.

Burgundian's owner had a delightful wife and a daughter of about my age and I was invited to stay the night with them which I was very happy to do.

I think Biddy and I went over to Frithville two or three times, staying the night and spending the following day with them before Biddy decided she would tolerate her handsome suitor as a mate. I know that we were very elated when that occurred – we all had a celebratory drink and Biddy had another feed of oats! We were so pleased Biddy had stopped being so churlish with the partner I had chosen for her.

The following day I rode Biddy gently back to her riverside field at Tattershall Bridge. Periodically I would cycle over to have a chat with her and ask how she felt. Did she feel like eating coal or had she any other unusual urges? Did she want any knitting done? Not surprisingly Biddy was entirely non-committal and neither by looks nor behaviour could I gain an inkling as to whether or not she was definitely carrying a foal. However, by the following Spring she was obviously in foal and getting bigger by the day. I often wondered what the temperament of this forthcoming foal was likely to be and how it how it would mature. For, from what I could gather about Burgundian's offspring they "would rather go about on two legs than four – and they didn't mind which pair they used". Problems ahead!

Fortunately my sister at Leadenham had kindly agreed to have Bridget on their farm to foal. My problem was how to get Bridget from Coningsby to Leadenham as no transport was available and I could not ride her when she was due to foal in a few short weeks time. I decided that I would lead her from my ancient trusty Raleigh bicycle. A day was set for this expedition and I arranged to meet Ken in Lincoln that evening at a Dance after Biddy had been left at Leadenham to foal.

All went well for the first few miles as Biddy trotted briskly beside my bicycle. She then became bored and refused to go any faster than a walk. So there was I, in WAAF uniform, leading a heavily pregnant mare at walking pace from a bicycle through small country villages. The comments which came my way from onlookers were quite embarrassing. Some even thought Biddy might foal there and then! Time was passing and I was rapidly becoming more and more behind in my schedule for the day. At length I could bear the strain no longer. I felt I simply had to telephone my sister, for moral support, if nothing else.

It was never advisable to tie Bridget up outside the stable, for if she pulled back and felt herself restrained, she panicked and used all her strength to break free, resulting in a broken bridle or headcollar and a loose horse. Nevertheless, I was desperate and looped Biddy's reins around a telegraph pole on the roadside and quickly pedalled away to find a telephone box in the nearby village hoping that during my absence Biddy wouldn't break free and disappear back the way we had come – back to Coningsby. When I eventually pushed Button "A" in the telephone kiosk and heard my sister speak, tears of relief rolled down my cheeks and I could hardly speak coherently. Ivy said that she and Joy, her daughter, would saddle up as quickly as possible and ride out to meet me as Bridget could be led more easily and willingly from another horse as they are herd animals and always go better in company than alone.

The Gods were with me – I was able to retrieve Biddy from the telegraph post and at walking pace we slowly continued on our way. At last a ridden horse and pony appeared in the distance. Biddy pricked up her ears with interest and increased her pace as the distance between us and the riders shortened. In fact, when we met and I had handed her reins over to Joy to lead from her pony Biddy said she had never felt fitter in her life and wanted to make a race of it to Leadenham. It was all I could do to keep up with them as I pedalled as fast as I could in pursuit of the three horses and two riders – they were either trotting fast or cantering as Biddy tried to lead them at a headlong gallop for the remainder of the journey.

I can't remember if I ever did have the time or the energy to go to a Dance that night with Ken. Biddy was certainly a nightmare that day.

*Action shots of Sylvia and Bridget
taken to try out Dr. Maiden's new camera.*

14. *Letters from Bob Owens*

I unearthed these letters August, 1997 and, after a gap of over 50 years, deeply regret that I cannot remember the writer! We must have met during that unhappy time when I was Clerk to the Senior Medical Officer at R.A.F. Base Station, Coningsby, Lincolnshire. One of my duties was to arrange parades at Station Sick Quarters for "jabs" against Tetanus and T.B. Perhaps members of the R.A.F. Regiment stationed at R.A.F. Coningsby were amongst my "victims" and I got into conversation with him there – he obviously knew the size and whereabouts of my office – and he also knew that my mare, Bridget, was in foal. I did not attend any social events at the Camp when I was off duty at S.S.Q., so we could not have met socially.

I am amused by the PS of Bob's letter where he says "I'd put a kiss, but have not yet been out with you <u>seven</u> times". This reminds me that I had my own rule that I would not go out with anyone just because they wanted to have a "snog" or petting session! No matter how much I liked them, I would not kiss them goodnight until we had been out several times together without kissing! I thought the figure was probably three – perhaps five – but surely <u>seven</u> was rather excessive? Perhaps he chose a higher number just to tease me? I wonder! In the letter following this one he did say, "but then little Curlilocks was always a most unusual Waaf".

I won't argue with that.

In Bob's letter of the 4th July, 1943 he writes: "so that little prop is worth an extra 4d. per day. Robbery I calls it".

I had recently been successful in taking examinations to be promoted from Aircraftwoman 1st Class to Leading Aircraftwoman, so I would have had a small cloth propeller badge to sew on the sleeve of my jacket to indicate my new rank and had 4d per day increase in pay. So, each fortnightly Pay Day I should receive an extra 52½ n.p.

We seem to have enjoyed teasing each other a lot and got on very well together – and he was surprised and pleased that I wrote to him, as most members of the R.A.F. Regiment had the reputation of being rather a tough lot, not renowned for their "drawing-room" behaviour. Nevertheless, I did have another R.A.F. Regiment friend – LAC Wally Smith. I was at R.A.F. Hospital Rauceby for an eye operation (21st April, 1943-5th May, 1943) and Wally kindly made his way over there more than once to take me walking round the grounds, as my eyes were completely bandaged and he gave me his support when I needed it, as I don't think I had any other visitors whilst I was there – my mother had died two months previously. Wally had a fiancée back at home so we behaved very properly but he was there when I needed someone to befriend me, for which I was grateful as I was so desperately unhappy at S.S.Q. (I was surprised to find how difficult it is to recognise what one is eating when you have chased some unknown food around the plate for some time before "capturing" it and putting it in your mouth. I hadn't realised before how much "sight" influences "taste".)

To return to Bob's letters, I don't know what the "news about your dearly beloved F/Sgt" was. I 100% disliked the one in charge at S.S.Q. At the foot of Bob's letter he says: "Give my regards to Charles". I wonder who he was?

Bob seems to have written to me eight times between 3.6.43 and 1.7.43 which is well over one a week and I had written the same number of times to him. Then the letters just stopped. I did not get the information on London Shows he was going to obtain for me. Did the R.A.F. Regiment have another "two hour posting" – as happened when they left R.A.F. Coningsby?

"We get one 32 hour Pass every twelve days but can't leave camp apart from that."

Sounds as if they were likely to be sent off somewhere at very short notice.

I wonder what happened to Bob and if he is still alive or did something horrible happen, as was so often the case in wartime? I shall probably never know…

> *1425526 LAC OWENS, F.R.*
>
> *R.A.F. Regiment Station, Foreness,*
>
> *Nr MARGATE, Kent*
>
> *Friday*

My Dear Sylvia,

Please excuse me for giving you such a shock but I've just indulged in a two hour posting. Shakes the troops doesn't it. My address in future will be as above. I'm sorry there is no news to tell you but things have been extremely quiet – apart from one shell – and I hope they will keep that way for a nice long time. I hope you are having a decent time these days and not getting thoroughly cheesed off! I'm still managing to keep all our 295's[1] organised – hope to obtain ten days leave on the 20th.

Must close now but will write again soon.

Keep smiling,

Yours Bob

---

[1] Leave Form

1425526 LAC OWENS, F.R.

2808 Squadron,

R.A.F. Station, Dunkirk,

Nr. FAVERSHAM, Kent

Thursday 3/6/43

Dear Sylvia,

I hope that an airman – especially in the RAFR[1] – keeping a promise to write won't shock you too much. Coningsby would certainly look good after this dump but everybody is pretty cheerful. I hope you are feeling better by now and not missing those noisy Regiment boys. I guess we left enough behind to keep you occupied for some time to come.

Please accept my most humble apologies for not saying much on Wednesday morning but I was suffering from a bad dose of the blues. Sorry I couldn't stay longer to keep you company and hope you won't think too badly of me when next you see a crow-bar.

Keep smiling,

Yours, Bob

R.A.F. Foreness

Saturday

My Dear Joan,

Many many thanks for your letter which arrived this afternoon. It sure is grand to know that someone remembers yours platonically. How are you these days. I seem to be in a permanently browned off state. It sure would take a damned good detective to find any attractions in this dump. How about getting posted down here? I could do with a typist to help fill the office up.

---

[1] Royal Air Force Regiment

I think I had better describe this super splendid office of mine. Just imagine a big wooden hut about three times the size of your office and with somewhere about half a dozen phones in it – no two!!! big tables. The officer sits at one and I sit at t'other and we write or read just as we feel. I start work at 08.45 and finish at about 17.30 There's not a day goes by without I finish work by about 10.00 and then I just sit and wait for the Naafi and the Red Shield. I've been to the pictures this evening to see "Wake Island" and have thoroughly enjoyed myself.

Rather reminded me of Foreness by moonlight. It certainly sounds as if you've been losing some beauty sleep lately. You'd better come here and catch up on some. Just imagine my having to be in by 22.30 Sorry to hear that my letters have been becoming steadily more sarcastic. Please let me know if there is any improvement in this letter. I'm crossing my fingers and hoping hard. I'll not pass any remarks about your triping, Sylvia. I'll just send an eraser. O.K? I take an exceedingly dim view of a certain Leading aircraftwench who not only cooks the suppers but her fingers also. Clumsy brute! Any comments. S'wizard to be able to imagine you doing a crafty double after Giddy Biddy. Serve you right for laughing so much at the R.A.F.R.

How's she going to get the coupons for the little woollen horseshoes?

Must close now but will write again soon.

Cheerio for now,

Yours etc. etc., Bob

P.S. Hope the start of this didn't shake you too much. [1]

---

[1] My Christian names are Joan Sylvia—I have never used Joan. Don't know how he knew it.

1425526 LAC OWENS, F.R.

R.A.F. Regiment,

Foreness, Nr MARGATE

Sunday 4.6.43

My Dear Sylvia,

Many thanks for the last letter you sent to me. Please accept my apologies for the delay in answering same but I've been able to scrounge a crafty twenty four. Makes yer fink!! The weather here is grand and I've managed to get a few sun-bathing hours in. It sounds rather as if you've been busy lately. Makes a break from the monotony for you doesn't it. So that little prop is worth an extra 4d. Robbery I calls it. I guess its lucky I'm not around when you read this or I should be attending S.S.Q. for about a month. I was also very very pleased to find out that the second half of your letter could be read quite easily. S'wizard! You don't need a crash guard at Coningsby do you? I should be only too pleased to oblige. Any objections? I see you've got the right idea about sleep anyway. Nothing like it is there. Not that we get much normally although we've not been disturbed since I last wrote to you.

Sorry about the library books but you know yourself just what a truthful little man I am. Compared with me old George Washington was a narrator of terminological inexactitudes. Quiet, Sprog!

Don't go to sleep next time you go to Church either or I shall have to come back and liven you up somewhat. Sorry I can't write more now but am very busy.

Keep smiling,

Yours etc. etc. etc., Bob

P.S. I'd put a kiss but have not yet been out with you seven times. Bob.

P.P.S. Seems my hint on typing came in useful after all.

1425526 LAC OWENS, F.
R.A.F. Regiment,
R.A.F. Station, Foreness,
Nr Margate, Kent.
Monday, 14.6.1943

Dear Sprog,

Many many thanks for your letter which arrived this morning. It certainly is grand to hear from you and to know that you haven't forgotten me yet. How are you, Sylvia, still cheesed off with Coningsby? You sure would have plenty to be fed up with here. We get one thirty-two hour pass every twelve days but can't leave camp apart from that. Talk about liking to be beside the seaside.

I fail to see where the lack of sarcasm comes in but I guess I don't hear you nagging away all the time. Sorry! Believe me, Coningsby is lovely and I heartily wish I was back again. I've managed to get home for a couple of hours but my leave seems like my tapes. See what I mean? S'wizard! It's the first time that I've ever heard of a Waaf working hard enough to perspire, but, then, little Curlilocks was always a most unusual Waaf. That even goes for the ink.

Must close now for my ink supply seems to be getting rather low and I don't want to cut myself to finish this letter.

Be a good girl and hold your patient's hand and think of me.

Keep smiling, Bob

P.S. I don't know about "keep smiling" you will probably have a fit laughing when you've read what a place we've come to.

P.P.S. In my usual scrounging manner – am now <u>in charge</u> of the Orderly Room. Bags of passes maybe?

1425526 LAC OWENS, F.

R.A.F. Regt, R.A.F. Station, Foreness,

Nr Margate.

Tuesday, 22.6.43

Dear Sprog (LACW pending discharge),

Many humble apologies for writing this most marvellous epistle in pencil but during a brief leave (24 hrs) a certain gunner has done his best to paint the floor with my ink. I hope you are not working – and binding – too hard for that would never do. I mean to say that one has sometimes to think of the people one works with. Sorry! Now after such a glorious beginning I'll thank you very much for the letter received Monday morning. I thought you would have forgotten yours truly by now.

By the way is it pay day at Coningsby this week or has S.S.Q. managed to find some more ink? Its lucky you're not around or I would see me getting my eye in a sling.

I managed to scrounge a couple of hours at home from yesterday at three until this morning at nine. Not so bad. Talk about sun-tan, you should see the 295's getting organised. By the way, after sorting out the F's from the telegraph poles I've come to the conclusion that your letter should be framed as a masterpiece of sarcasm. Do you mind. It was news about your dearly beloved F/Sgt. but I rather pity the poor devil who has to work with you now.

Sorry I must close now but will write again soon.

Yours,

Frank

1425526 <u>LAC</u> OWENS, F. R.

R.A.F. Regiment,

R.A.F. Station, Foreness,

Nr Margate, Kent.

Saturday 26th June, 1943

Dear Senior L.A.C.W. (acting unpaid, unwanted),

Many many thanks for the very charming letter received from you this afternoon. It is so lovely to read such a letter and to realise that at last it contains no sarcasm. I can only think that your sweet nature must be coming to the rescue at long last. You can have no idea how much pleasure it would give me to use that long and bendy perspex ruler to good effect. If such a thing were possible dear little Sylvia would have a few bruises that she couldn't show her latest boyfriend. O.K?

You must excuse the size of this notepaper but with winter drawing closer I thought it might come in handy for lighting one or two fires in a Nissen hut. I'll also have to beg of you to excuse me if my writing becomes slightly shaky at times as the guns cause the table to vibrate occasionally.

So pleased to hear that Bridget at least can find her way home. Shows what a little horse-sense can do. (Pause to let it sink in).

By the way, is my writing school-girlish enough for you these days? You know me – always willing to oblige if I can get something out of it. So very pleased to hear that you have been able to get one respectable meal since you have been at Coningsby. You should come here and have three good meals and still be hungry. I don't know if I've mentioned it before but during the last fortnight or so we've developed a new way of spending our nights beside sleeping. You'll find an example below:

Scene: A Handicraft hut complete with six sleeping gunners.

Time: 02.00

Enter a corporal in a hurry and not much else.

Cpl: "For God's sake get outside, lads".

141

Lads: "Hoppit"

One shrill whistle is heard.

Result: Empty hut and bags of panic.

That's been happening quite a lot since we've been here and we've been quite accustomed to spending a couple of hours in a trench with a machine gun but now it is quieter and can remain so for all I care. Quite a change from dear old Coningsby anyway. One for the worse I'm afraid. Mind you I'd like to have myself a go and forget the 48's and 295's but he nearly always – touch wood – drops them in the sea and then everybody feels very very pleased.

I hope this letter isn't growing too binding but I've been sitting here all day and have finished my two library books and now badly need something to pass my time away.

If I were you I should learn to type before next attempting to address an envelope. You use your thumb for spacing not your third finger left hand. Quiet Sprog!!!

I'll close now,

Don't go to sleep in church again you lazy!!!

Keep smiling, Bob

Address as usual - Foreness.

Wednesday, 14th July, 1943

My Dear Country Bumpkin,

My most humble apologies for writing to you in pencil but my fountain pen became slightly squashed last night or I should say this morning. I guess you would too if nearly thirteen stone fell flat on top of you. Makes yer fink don't it. I was terribly pleased to get your letter this morning and nearly shed a few tears to hear of you working so hard. Please put in for my posting to S.S.Q. Coningsby as a typewriter tapper (LAC pending 10 days leave). Any comments? Now I'll tell you a tale of a shell. (Pause whilst my memory tries to function.)

It was 03.00 hours on a dark and dreary night. Joe Mug was sitting in a blue-pencil gun pit waiting for a Jerry who was probably comfortably in bed. He got rather a shock when there was a big bang and then heard a sound like the Boston express. Having looked, listened and hoped to see or hear a plane he was severely shaken to realise that he was sitting on the receiving end of a blinking great coastal gun. O.K? We've been disturbed slightly the last couple of nights but nothing much to speak of – touch wood. Hence the fountain pen and ink stained blouse.

Was terribly sorry to hear that you went out on the razzle the other night. You's better come to Margate and get stinko with me. By the way, if you have a job to decipher this scribble of mine, please return this and I'll order a typewritten copy. The powers that be have actually had the audacity to present me with a half share in one of ye olde and original Olivers.[1] They've got a !!!???!!! cheek to even own such a thing. I guess old Noah used it for making nominal rolls and 48's in the Ark.

Sorry I can't give you any information on London Shows but will make a few enquiries and let you know the results. The only ones I know are any good are:-

ADELPHI   "Dancing Years" by Ivor Novello

PALLADIUM   "Best Bib and Tucker" by George Black

COLISEUM   "It's Foolish but It's Fun"

Sorry I can't let you know of any more but will write and let you know soon.

Don't let that triping get you down.

Give my regards to Charles,

Frank

---

[1] Brand of typewriter

This is another letter which has lain hidden away for over fifty years and, as with the letters from Bob Owens of the R.A.F. Regiment, I regret I remember little about the writer.

I think Cyril Whiteoak was a Nursing Orderly at Station Sick Quarters R.A.F. Coningsby when I was a Clerk there. In his letter of 23.4.43 he refers to the occasion when he and I paid my only visit to Boston. I was then admitted to hospital hence the start of his letter to me.

I obtained from R.A.F. Innsworth, Gloucester copies of some of my Service details from which I see that I was admitted to R.A.F. Hospital Rauceby on 21st April, 1943 for an eye operation to try to correct my squint and was discharged on 2nd May, 1943. It seems that Cyril Whiteoak heard that I was in hospital and presumed I had been suddenly taken ill.

We probably did not meet again as he was posted to Station Sick Quarters Woodhall Spa, and I was just a few miles distant at Coningsby. Due to shortage of petrol travelling in wartime was never easy and we were well "out in the sticks" so hitch-hiking was out of the question. If we had both been on duty at S.S.Q. R.A.F. Coningsby things might well have been different.

1127091 LAC Whiteoak, C.

S.S.Q. R.A.F.,

Woodhall Spa, Lincoln

23.4.43

Dear Silvia,

Can you blame me for you being in hospital? I am very sorry to hear of you being taken ill so suddenly and taken from the fine surroundings of S.S.Q. Coningsby to be put into Rauceby Hospital.

But still it should be a rest for you to get away from that fatiguous and corrupt place and to have more pure surroundings where you are now.

If I am sent down into Ward I before you come out we may be able to see each other? Should you come across Cpl Lunn[1] please remember me to him. He may be nursing in Ward I as that was the purpose for which he was posted from Cranwell.

Last night I went to Boston, but this time all alone after I had been to the New Theatre and the Fighting Forces canteen. I met Vera and Ann, there are always S.S.Q. personnel in Boston it appears? I came back by the Woodhall bus which was almost empty, through the Squadron being away.

It was a fine change after being in here every night since last Sunday. I am feeling quite at home here now, much quieter than Coningsby.[2]

Miss Doe[3] will have the office to herself now for a short time, so your worry in that respect is now over. You may have the place to yourself when you come back? I think that you are very sincere and conscientious in the way that you think about that matter. More so by far than I think I am.

I hope you have a quick recovery and get the best of nursing, with plenty of fruit and all the best of food and company. Then I may have the pleasure of tormenting you again back at Coningsby.

Will you have a chance of sick leave, a little would do you no harm? You are not having the opportunity to look after Bridget. She is never going to have the pleasure of grazing in the fields of Tattershall.

I have done one or two water colour paintings at nights this last week. This is my best way of spending my time now.

---

[1] An ex Cranwellite

[2] R.A.F. Coningsby was the Base Station with two satellite stations— R.A.F. Woodhall Spa and R.A.F. East Kirkby

[3] Betty Doe was the very good natured Aircrafthand General Duties. She was one of the two WAAF ACH/GD's who, before my arrival, were on duty alternate nights.

I shall be pleased to see you healthy and well again.

All my best wishes for now,

I am your Sincere Friend,

Cyril

These letters from Bob and Cyril are included to illustrate the diversity of Service life, friendships and how they briefly entered and left one's life, often with very little notice.

15. *Fifty years on – news of Roo*

I believe I met Roo in December 1941 when returning on Bland's bus to camp from a trip into Oakham when Roo and I were both stationed at R.A.F. Cottesmore and we soon became great friends. I had almost completed my first year serving as a WAAF clerk to the Station Armament Officer and Sgt. Walter D. Langworthy was attending a course with a new nearly completed crew at the Operational Training Unit there. The crew of only five were training on the twin-engined Hampden or Wellington bombers. The final two members of their crew – the Flight Engineer and another gunner, would be picked up when they attended a Heavy Conversion Unit and converted from twin-engined aircraft to the four-engined Lancaster bomber.

I could not become enthusiastic about the name "Walter", so as he was an Australian, it seemed natural to nickname him "Roo", and as such he became known to my family and friends.

At the beginning of August, 1942 Roo began his operational flying in Lancasters which were based at R.A.F. Woodhall Spa. We met in Lincoln when possible and I tried to write to him daily whilst he was on ops. In February 1943 he came to support me at my Mother's funeral and that was the last time we had contact with each other, and the following month 97 Squadron was posted away from R.A.F. Woodhall Spa and I did not know where they went. I have recently been advised by Ann Savage, Hon. Sec. Of the newly-formed 97 (Straits Settlements) Squadron Association, that 97 Squadron left RAF Woodhall Spa for RAF Bourn, near Huntingdon, on 18th April 1943.

After I was demobbed I visited St Clement Danes Church in London, the Central Church of the Royal Air Force, to see if I could find Roo's name in the R.A.F. Memorial Book. I found that F/O W. D. Langworthy, D.F.C. was listed there as "killed in Action on 7th Jan. 1944". I naturally assumed that this had happened whilst on a bombing raid particularly when Ted Richardson told me that he had seen Roo's name on a Roll of Honour at Ely Cathedral where a window was dedicated on 6th November, 1955 "In memory of those members of aircrew of No. 8 Group Royal Air Force who flew on operational missions against the enemy from bases around Ely and did not return."

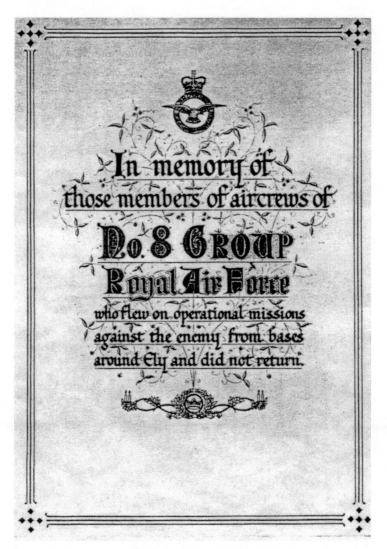

In memory of
those members of aircrews of
No. 8 Group
Royal Air Force
who flew on operational missions
against the enemy from bases
around Ely and did not return.

No 8 Group Roll of Honour

Rank	Name	Squadron	Date
F/Sgt	LAMBERT, J.	7	22nd Mar. 1944
F/O	LAMBERT, W. T., D.F.M.	109	23rd Dec. 1944
W/O	LAMONBY, J.	7	20th May 1944
Sgt.	LAMPEN, L. C.	105	11th April 1943
F/O	LAMPIN, F. E.	156	14th Jan. 1944
Sgt.	LANCASTER, E.	635	26th Aug. 1944
Sgt.	LANE, E. A.	405	14th Jan. 1944
Sgt.	LANE, R. M.	97	31st Mar. 1944
P/O	LANGFORD, D., D.F.C.	156	24th June 1944
P/O	LANGFORD, V.A.R.	83	20th Feb. 1944
F/Lt	LANGHAM, D. F., D.F.C.	7	15th Feb. 1944
F/O	LANGWORTHY, W. D., D.F.C.	1655MTU	7th Jan. 1944
F/Sgt	LAPTHORNE, L. N.	156	3rd Jan. 1944
W/O	LARKINS, A. R. P.	156	8th June 1944
P/O	LARSON, R. H.	405	17th Nov. 1943
F/O	LASCELLES, J. H., D.F.M.	156	3rd Feb. 1945
F/Sgt	LAURIE, L. G.	97	29th Jan. 1944
Sgt.	LAVER, L. N. J.	97	14th Jan. 1944
Sgt.	LAVERICK, W., D.F.M.	35	29th Dec. 1943
F/O	LAW, A. C.	405	10th July 1943
F/O	LAW, N. C.	97	30th Jan. 1944
F/Sgt	LAW, R. G.	7	8th Aug. 1944
F/Sgt	LAWLEY, R.	635	31st Mar. 1944
W/O	LAWRANCE, C. H., D.F.M.	156	14th Jan. 1944
F/Sgt	LAWRENCE, A. G.	7	20th May 1944
W/O2	LAWRENCE, A. K.	405	14th Jan. 1944
Sgt.	LAWRENCE, R. A.	97	17th Dec. 1943
F/O	LAWRENCE, W. J.	405	23rd Nov. 1943
F/Lt	LAWSON, C. D.	405	16th June 1943
F/O	LAWSON, G. S.	35	23rd Dec. 1944
W/C	LAWSON, K. J., D.S.O. AND BAR, D.F.C.	405	2nd Jan. 1945
F/Sgt	LAWSON, R.	7	4th Sept. 1943
F/O	LAWTON, E. E.	97	29th June 1943
F/Sgt	LAY, K. L. W.	156	11th June 1943
F/Lt	LAYLEY, R. G.	7	14th Jan. 1944
P/O	LAYTON-SMITH, M. S.	7	19th Aug. 1944
Sgt.	LEADER, J. L.	156	27th July 1943
F/O	LEADER, R. A.	635	11th April 1944
F/Sgt	LEAHY, A. F. G.	7	22nd Mar. 1944
P/O	LEATHERDALE, C. G.	156	31st Mar. 1944
S/L	LEATHERLAND, D.	97	21st April 1944
F/Sgt	LEAVESLEY, W. D.	405	16th Sept. 1944
F/Sgt	LEBIHAN, G. E. J.	405	28th May 1943
Sgt.	LECOMBER, J. E.	83	13th May 1943
Sgt.	LEDGER, R. V.	35	2nd Mar. 1943
F/O	LEE, E. V.	156	27th July 1943
W/O1	LEE, J. L.	35	30th May 1943
P/O	LEE, R. J.	156	5th May 1943
F/Sgt	LEVEY, J.		
F/O	LEVIN, M. H. O., D		
F/O	LEWIS, A.		
Sgt.	LEWIS, B. E.		
F/O	LEWIS, F. E.		
F/O	LEWIS, G. W.		
Sgt.	LEWIS, H.		
Sgt.	LEWIS, H. J.		
F/O	LEWIS, J. W.		
Sgt.	LEWIS, L. A.		
F/Sgt	LEWIS, R. C. L.		
F/Sgt	LEWIS, S. J. R.		
F/Sgt	LEWIS, V. C., D		
F/Sgt	LIDDLE, S. M.		
Sgt.	LIDDLE, T. B.		
Sgt.	LIDSTER, E.		
F/Sgt	LIGHTFOOT-SHANDLEY, E.		
W/O1	LINDSAY, B. E.		
Sgt.	LINDSAY, W.		
Sgt.	LINEHAM, W. A.		
F/O	LINTON, A., D.		
Sgt.	LISSNER, P. R.		
Sgt.	LISTER, G. P.		
F/Sgt	LISTER, H. A.		
W/O	LITTLE, A.		
Sgt.	LITTLE, D. H. W		
F/O	LITTLE, G. J.		
Sgt.	LITTLE, J.		
W/O	LITTLE, J. F.		
F/Lt	LITTLE, S. W.		
F/Lt	LIVELY, F.		
P/O	LIVINGSTON, R. A.,		
F/Sgt	LLOYD, W. D. L		
S/L	LOBB, H. C., D.F		
Sgt.	LOBB, R.		
F/Sgt	LOCK, L. G. K.		
W/C	LOCKHART, W D.S.O., D.F.C. AN		
F/O	LOCKWOOD, F,		
F/Lt	LOCKYER, C. C.		
F/Lt	LODER, G. B.,		
F/O	LOFTUS, W. T.,		
Sgt.	LOGAN, J. A.		
P/O	LOGAN, R. H.		
F/Lt	LONG, R. W., D.		
P/O	LONG, S. H.		
F/Sgt	LONG-HARTLE		
W/C	LONGFIELD, G.		
F/Sgt	LONGLAND, G.		
F/Sgt	LONSDALE, G.		
F/O	LOPEZ, R. H.		
W/O	LORD, J.		
P/O	LORD, M.		

33

List of names taken from Roll of Honour

150

I recently asked John Larder for any comments about why "97" left 5 Group and these are his thoughts on the matter:

"Without doubt 5 Group was the elite, mainly due to its commander Cochrane, who to many observers was the outstanding Group commander and probably should have replaced Harris after the Battle of Berlin. Within that exalted company, "83" and "97" Squadrons were chosen to go to 8 Group as Pathfinders which is proof of their reputations."

Subsequently Ted found out for me that Roo was not on ops when he was killed but on a training flight in a Mosquito of 1655 Mosquito Training Flight from R.A.F. Marham in Norfolk, with F/Lt Jolly as the pilot, when the plane crashed at Llangstone Court in Herefordshire at 1530 hours on 7th January, 1944, having taken off from Marham an hour earlier. Both occupants were killed when the Mosquito exploded and burst into flames before crashing.

Ted also obtained a copy of the Accident Report for me which stated: "Explosion in mid-air, after loss of control aircraft disintegrated. Pilot blown out without a chute. Navigator baled out. Aircraft on fire after explosion." "Flame trap set screw trapped in valve – hot gases burned valve seating – backfiring – blew out supercharger. No fault of crew". "Aircraft disintegrated in stress of loss of control plus engine fire." "AIB (Air Investigation Board): Engine failure in air with subsequent loss of control, aircraft broke up in air."

According to the Accident Report F/Lt Jolly, the pilot, was a New Zealander of great experience who had flown 2,170 solo hours on nine different types of aircraft. He was buried at St. Albans on 12th January, 1944 and the Unit was represented by the local R.A.F. Units and 1519 B.A.T. Flight, Feltwell, Norfolk where he had been C.O. F/O W. D. Langworthy D.F.C. was my friend "Roo" whom I met at 14 O.T.U. R.A.F. Cottesmore in December, 1941. On the 11th January, 1944 F/O Langworthy was buried at R.A.F. Cemetery at Haycombe, Bath; the Unit was represented by F/Lt F. Griggs and Padre Sands from R.A.A.F. Headquarters.

Ted Richardson very kindly put a request in a local paper to see if anyone remembered the crash of over fifty years ago. To my surprise and delight this is a copy of the letter I received:

March, 1995

Dear Mrs. Watts,

I am writing ref your letter about the Mosquito that crashed at Llangstone Court, Llangarron 7th January, 1944. So sorry to hear that it was your friend. We remember it well. I heard a loud explosion and thought it was an aircraft that had blown up. I made my way to Llangstone Court. In a lane close by was one of the engines. The main part of the plane came down in a field close by. When I got there it was burnt out but still smouldering. But there were parts scattered over several fields. I was told the two people in the plane were killed. My wife remembers it more than I do because we met at the crash and have been married for 45 years. I was in the R.A.F. from 1946-1948 National Service.

I hope this will help you.

Yours sincerely,

Stanley and Mary

P.S. A letter was passed on to me from Mr. Richardson of Nottingham asking for the same information, also tells me F/O Langworthy, D.F.C. is buried in Bath.

13th February, 1999

Dear Mrs. Watts,

... I had to go to Hereford yesterday and went into the library to see if I could see the local papers which they had at the library but no mention of the plane crash.

I have also been talking to a man whose house was on the edge of one of the fields where the plane crashed, parts of the plane landed on his lawn and garden. He says he remembers it well although he wasn't at home when it crashed. He is over 90.

I asked him if he knew if there was a marker[1] anywhere. He said no, as the plane was scattered over several fields, and there was a body found in the next field. He also told me the R.A.F. stayed by his house in a tent for about 5 weeks after the crash cleaning up. He remembers them cooking a nice meal for him and his family before they left...

❖ ❖ ❖

Extract from a letter dated 12th March, 1999:

...I was talking to a gentleman who worked on the farm where the body was found. He said that he was wearing a parachute but it was coming down very fast. The wife thinks the plane was too low and the parachute was damaged.

In May, 1999 Stan and Mary forwarded photographs Mary had taken of the crash site explaining the areas where the various parts of the Mosquito were found.

---

[1] As a memorial

Plane crashed in this field

Propeller on this road on the lane, also second engine wedged by the tree on the top of the bank. This is where Mary and Stan met.

Operational trips of Aus. 408157 F/O W.D. Langworthy, D.F.C.
No. 97 Lancaster Bomber Squadron
Ops Nos. 1-17: Pilot – F/Sgt G. A. West

No.	Date	Target	Comments
1	3-4th Aug 1942	Gardening	Forget me not
2	6-7th Aug 1942	Duisburg	
3	9-10th Aug 1942	Gardening	Radish
4	11-12th Aug 1942	Mainz	
5	18-19th Sept 1942	Gardening	Sweet Pea
6	23-24th Sept 1942	Wismar	
7	13-14th Oct 1942	Kiel	
8	8-9th Nov 1942	Gardening	Deodars
9	13-14th Nov 1942	Genoa	
10	17-17th Nov 1942	Gardening	Pollack
11	4-5th Dec 1942	Gardening	Spinach
12	6-7th Dec 1942	Mannheim	
13	9-10th Dec 1942	Turin	
14	21-22 Dec 1942	Munich	
15	31-1st Jan 1943	Gardening	Lost escape hatches. Op aborted
16	7-8 Jan 1943	Essen	Commissioned 29/1/43
17	9-10th Jan 1943	Essen	

I include a map John Larder found for me which details the code names for the areas in which mine laying operations took place. Roo appears to have taken part in six of these operations while based at R.A.F. Woodhall Spa with 97 Squadron. In a letter John informed me that:

"the arrival of Roo with Flt/Sgt West was probably fairly accidental and either he was assigned to West who kept him thereafter in the crew or he may have gone to the Squadron to replace West's existing navigator.

Flt Sgt West finished his tour at Essen after thirty-one trips on 9/10th January, 1943 and was nominated for the Distinguished Flying Medal on 25th January, 1943 and it appeared in the London Gazette on 12th March, 1943. In the Citation for his D.F.M. it states 'on one occasion Flt Sgt West flew his aircraft back to this country in very adverse conditions following an attack by an enemy fighter. This action saved the lives of the injured members of the crew.' It seems likely that this occurred on the trip to Munich on 21/22nd December, 1942 as there were some crew changes after that raid which may have denoted crew injuries."

Jim Wright tells me that he found the following at the Public Records Office, Kew under file reference AIR 27/766:

"Pilot's debriefing report on Munich raid 21/22. Dec. 42. Time up: 1734 his. Time down: 0015 his. Thin cloud, good visibility. When we reached Munich bombed with 13 SBCs with target in bombsights. Own bombs not seen to burst but several large fires seen in built-up areas. Aircraft damaged by flak and fighters. Extent of damage not ascertained Crew worked well together after being shot up. Three crew members injured. Landed at Watton. "

He was commissioned and after probably a spell instructing at an Operational Training Unit returned to ops with 44 Squadron and was killed in the battle of Berlin on the night of 23rd December, 1943 on the ninth op. of his second tour. He is buried in Berlin in the 1939-45 War Cemetery.

18	12-13 Jan 1943	Essen	
19	16-17th Jan 1943	Berlin	
20	17-18th Jan 1943	Berlin	
21	30-31 Jan 1943	Hamburg	
22	2/3 Feb 1943	Cologne	
23	13-14th Feb 1943	Lorient	
24	14-15th Feb 1943	Milan	

25	18-19th Feb 1953	Wilhelmshaven	Posted to 16 OUT 13.3.43
26	21-22nd Feb 1942	Bremen	Upper Heyford
27	26-27th Feb 1943	Cologne	Posted to 1665 MTU (Marham)
28[1]	28-1st March 1943	St Nazaire	07/12/43

Roo had only completed seventeen ops of his tour when he flew on Flt Sgt West's last op of his first tour which was to Essen on 9/10th January, 1943. However, there was no delay before Roo joined a new crew for three days later on 12/13 January, 1943 he was flying as navigator to P/O R. R. Culenaere on an op to Essen once again. I had heard that P/O Culenaere had completed two tours and returned to his native Canada. Hoping that he might still be alive so that I could ask him about his memories of Roo who was his navigator for ten ops between 12th January, 1943 and 1st March, 1943 I put an advert in a Canadian magazine. It appeared in "Vapour Trails" in April, 2000 but I had no replies. At the end of May, 2001 I was surprised and delighted to receive the following card dated 23rd May, 2001 from Fred Dashper in Canada in which Fred said:

'...I was looking at the Summer 2000 issue of Airforce magazine and noticed your request for information on M. R. Culenaere formerly of 97 Sqdn. RAF. I imagine that you have heard from someone by now regarding your inquiry but in case you haven't I thought that I would advise you that Cully died sometime prior to February 1996. I last saw him at a Wartime Pilot's reunion in Winnipeg in 1988.

Cully and I trained together at Upper Heyford OTU in 1942 before being posted to different Squadrons. He went to 97 and I went to 61 Squadron. He was a good friend. I believe he is survived by his widow."

---

[1] Only 28 sorties listed, but D.F.C. citation says "sorties 32, flying hours 199".

I wrote to her, but not surprisingly had no reply.

In a subsequent letter Fred wrote:

"I wish you every success with your book as I am sure it will be very interesting. I look forward to obtaining a copy. I have enjoyed hearing from you and am sure that a story from the WAAF's point of view will be very interesting. Please let me know when it will be available."

I was interested to see that when Roo finished his tour with "Cully" as his pilot, he went to Upper Heyford on instructional duties which was where "Cully" and Fred Dashper had both trained. Roo was posted from 16 O.T.U. Upper Heyford to 1655 M.T.U. on 7th December, 1943 when the following report was made on him:

"This officer has been most useful to this Unit as he was a strong personality and possesses considerable `drive' and has done a splendid job on the satellite with a minimum of supervision. " (signed) W/Cdr G. F. Rodney.

No. of hours flown as an Observer 530 of which 33 his flown during the last 6 months.

Roo looked very smart in his officer's uniform when he came to my Mother's funeral in February, 1943; he had only been commissioned a few weeks earlier on 29th January, 1943.

I saw from Roo's list of ops that he was posted to R.A.F. Marham not far from Kings Lynn on 7th December, 1943 to 1655 M.T.U. in preparation for a second tour of ops.

As I was not Roo's next of kin it has been extremely difficult to obtain any details about his record. Neither R.A.F. Marham nor 1655 M.T.U. could help and 97 Squadron has never had a Squadron Association after the end of hostilities. So it is not known for sure why Roo was sent to 1655 Mosquito Training Unit. I asked John Larder for his ideas about a M.T.U. and he wrote:

"a navigator in a Mosquito was navigator, wireless op. and part flight engineer, so it was a bit different from life in a Lancaster. In view of his being commemorated at Ely I would guess that he was destined for the Light Night Striking Force or Pathfinders."

My ex-WAAF colleague, Beryl, advertised for information for me and was sent a lot of details by an Australian which included the following kit list and the fact that Roo went to Buckingham Palace on 21st October, 1943 to receive his D.F.C.

PERSONAL EFFECTS OF THE LATE AUS. 408157 – F/O W. D. LANGWORTHY (D.F.C.)

1	D.F.C. Medal and Ribbon*	1	pr. Nail scissors
88	Photos	1	Housewife
1	**Steel trunk (damaged) containing:**	2	black leather wallets
1	Attache case	1	red leather wallet
11	blue collars	1	Radio valve
4	blue shirts	1	Craft Masonry Hand-book
7	Singlets	11	keys on ring
1	Officers Greatcoat	5	Electrical fittings
1	Wool Dressing gown	1	leather tobacco pouch
4	Suits pyjamas	2	Pipes
1	Pyjama jacket	1	rubber dog Bone
4	prs. Drawers	1	dog collar
2	Towels	1	shoe horn
41	Handkerchiefs	1	bottle opener

* D.F.C. M. & R. extracted and forwarded by Reg. Post 3.1.45 (D.F.C. medals and ribbons)

40	only socks	1	toilet bag
4	Face washers	1	pencil sharpener in case
2	prs. Wool stockings	1	metal tie clip
1	pr. K. D. stockings	3	metal brooches
4	Wool pullovers	1	Pony Club Badge
1	Beret	2	clothes brushes
1	Balaclava	2	cycle lamps
1	Linen Bag	1	R.S.L. wallet
2	Wool scarves	1	brown leather writing case
1	Blue raincoat	1	Trigonometry book
1	Pillow slip	1	Hair brush
1	Airman blue tunic (O badge attached)	1	Address Book
2	Officers Blue Tunic (O Badge, D.F.C. 1939/43 Ribbons attached)	1	stamp album containing stamps
3	prs. Black shoes	2	Accounts Books
1	Thimble	1	Parker Fountain Pen W.D.L.
1	pr. leather slippers	1	Photo Album (empty)
1	pr. Sand shoes	1	Diary
2	F. S. caps & badges	1	Nail file
1	S.D. cap & Badge	1	black purse
3	prs. Leather gloves	1	Swan Fountain Pen
2	Black ties	1	bdle Pamphlets
1	Compass	2	Masonic Lodge Books
3	Portraits in frames	3	Sheets of Music
3	prs. Braces	13	Photos
2	Combs	1	Dictionary
1	**Blue fibre suit case containing:**	19	Books
2	cycle pumps	4	Booklets
4	Tooth brushes	2	Letters
1	Safety razor in tin	2	Cables
1	cycle repair Outfit	2	Greeting cards

I am particularly touched by seeing the items '1 dog collar' and '1 rubber bone'. These must have belonged to the little stray terrier, "Jackass" he took back to R.A.F. Woodhall Spa from Leadenham (for details see my letter home of 24th June, 1942) and who enjoyed flying with several crews – and then disappeared. I think the Pony Club badge was probably mine.

Gardening Map (1)

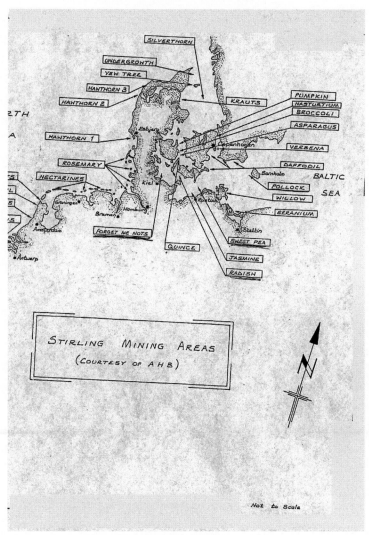

Gardening Map (2)

Stan and Mary sent me a copy of their local paper, the *Ross Gazette*, 1st June, 2000 in which the following extracts appeared:

'A fatal accident which took place at Llangarron in 1944 resulted in a remarkable story of love and friendship, much of which occurred as a result of the tragedy.

… As it was still wartime when the accident happened, and even though the aircraft was not downed by enemy action, such crashes, whatever the cause, would be kept secret, and only the RAF and the local residents would have been aware of what had happened.

… Stan was sixteen at the time. He walked out from his home at Llangarron to the site of the crash sometime after it had happened.

The tragedy made a big impression on the young man – but he was not to know how involved in the story he would become.

Stan had other things on his mind at the time because he met a pretty girl called Mary, who had cycled out with her friend to the scene of the crash.

… Among the sad list of clothes and personal belongings, including his DFC, listed after the accident, were "1 rubber dog bone and 1 dog collar".

… It was ironic that two heroes who had survived so many sorties against the enemy should perish because of faulty mechanism.'

And from the edition of 29th June, 2000:

'At the time Stan was working as a conductor on the buses and he discovered that the girl was called Mary and she was working at Tretire.

They were married in St. Weonard's Church in 1950 after a seven year courtship.

By this time Stan was a bus driver and a collection was made by his regular passengers.

They raised £7, which was a very useful amount.

All the names of the people who gave money were listed in a little exercise book which Mary still keeps.'

Mary and Stan, who celebrated their
Golden Wedding in July 2000

It was with delight that I learned of the romance of Stan and Mary which bloomed from their meeting at the site of such tragedy. In our continuing correspondence Stan and Mary informed me of the celebration of their Golden wedding anniversary showing their life together continues to blossom.

In 1996 Norman Small (ex 460 RAAF Squadron Bomb Aimer) of Ouyen, Australia arranged, on my behalf, the following inscription to be put on the R.A.A.F. Memorial at Brisbane which had been erected as part of the RAAF's 75 Anniversary and was inaugurated on 2nd May.

'F/O W. D. LANGWORTHY, D.F.C.
A WONDERFUL FRIEND, STILL REMEMBERED
1996 SYLVIA WAAF'

I was eventually successful in obtaining official news of Roo's death and of his citation for the D.F.C. as this letter dated 3rd June, 1998 from the Ministry of Defence at Great Scotland Yard shows – at last I was able to find out the citation for his D.F.C:

"... Thank you for your letter of the 16 May 1998 concerning Flying Officer Walter Dinnathorne Langworthy AUS408157 who lost his life on 7 January 1944 whilst serving with the Royal Air Force.

Our surviving records show that Fg Off Langworthy was Navigator aboard Mosquito DZ356 operating with 1655 Mosquito Training Unit. On 7 January 1944 the crew of DZ356 were tasked with a training flight. At 1530 hours an engine failure in the air subsequently resulted in loss of control of the aircraft and an explosion, the aircraft crashing at Langstone Court, Llangarron, Herefordshire. Sadly, Fg Off Langworthy and the Pilot, Flt Lt K. F. Jolly 88240, both lost their lives.

Please find enclosed a copy of the citation for the Distinguished Flying Cross, awarded to W D Langworthy in May 1943.

CITATION: D.F.C.

*(143)   Pilot Officer Walter Dinnathorne LANGWORTHY
(Aus.408157), Royal Australian Air Force, No. 97
Squadron. (Navigator; sorties 32; flying hours 199.) As
navigator Pilot Officer Langworthy has completed
many successful sorties against very heavily defended
targets in Germany and Italy. On one occasion he had
a narrow escape when his seat in the aircraft was rid-
dled by bullets. The aircraft was badly damaged and 3
members of the crew were wounded. With great cool-
ness, Pilot Officer Langworthy not only navigated the
badly disabled aircraft back to this country but also
rendered effective aid to the wounded. His courage and
skill have always been above praise.*

It was a truly wonderful surprise to receive from Stan and
Mary in April 2001 the following article taken from the *Ross
Gazette*:

Too close for comfort

WAR-TIME EVACUEE *Sylvia Mandeville, née Bee Abraham con-
tacted The Ross Gazette after reading the account of the
aircraft which crashed with devastating consequences for the
pilot and crew in Llangarron in 1944.*

*Sylvia, and her sister Diana, were playing in the very field that
the plane came down in and have clear memories of that day.*

Sylvia hopes that her memories of that fateful day, January 7th, 1944, will be of interest to our readers.

There were only a few days left of the winter holidays. It was a clear day with blue skies so my sister Diana and Jill Webb the farmer's daughter and I ran out to play in the field below Garron Hill Farm. After a while my sister ran back to climb a pear tree in the garden.

Jill and I remained playing beneath an old elm tree. We knew we were doing wrong. We had been warned many times of the danger of elm trees and how they will drop a branch with no warning. But we played on, alert for any creaking in the branches above us.

It was then tense, disobedient, every nerve stretched and anticipating danger that we heard the sound.

The noise roared through the sky seconds before we saw the cause of it, a flaming ball bellowing through the sky, scattering sheets of metal like petals in spring.

A parachute, unopened, plummeted to the ten acre field beyond.

Grabbing our toys we ran. We ran from the tree as the plane twisted and contorted itself above us. We could see its number.

"It's coming down here" I cried.

Fear ran us over the field to the gate. In a frozen moment the molten metal crashed into the grass beneath the elm. A heavy wheel from the plane went thump-thumping down the slope on its own.

Then we were through the gate, crying and screaming to be comforted.

People, cars, soldiers, police all appeared as if a button had been pressed.

Mr. Webb called out: "I'll get the door of the chicken hutch!"
Later we saw a blanketed body being taken away on that
makeshift stretcher.

For some time the farm was the centre of attention. Soldiers
camped in the field guarding the wreckage. Important people
came and went. We children calmed down a little. School be-
gan and life returned to normal. On the face of it everything
was alright. But for many years, whenever I heard the drone of
a plane overhead, I would pause and wait, tense and anxious,
for the engine to stall and I would wait to hear the heavy wheel
to go on its thudding journey once again.

Mr. Brian Davies, Hon. Sec. of the Hereford and the Marches
Branch of the Aircrew Association and Stan, with the support
of the new Vicar of Tregarron, are arranging for a suitably engraved stone to be placed in Tregarron Church to make a
permanent memorial. Details of the crash which caused the
death of two very brave men – my great friend Roo and his
pilot F/Lt Jolly, nearly sixty years ago, will be displayed
nearby.

Ted Richardson kindly took this photo of Roo's grave at the R.A.F. cemetery at Haycombe, Bath for me as well as saying a little prayer and placing a small cross there.

Appendix I: *WAAF Reception Centres*

I have always been puzzled as to why I went to Harrogate to enlist in the WAAF, as I have never met anyone else who went there for that purpose. Beryl Williams, the WAAF Association Magazine Editor, has very kindly explained to me where and when the different WAAF Reception Centres operated.

This is what she said:

"Pre-war West Drayton was a Reception Centre for airmen and also became the Centre for WAAF in October, 1939. As it was not really suitable for them, when the air raids on London increased, the WAAF were moved to Harrogate in September, 1940 and most of the girls were billeted at the Grand Hotel. When recruitment increased Harrogate became No. 1 WAAF Depot. No. 2 WAAF Depot was opened at Innsworth in January, 1941. In May 1941 No. 1 Depot moved from Harrogate to Bridgnorth, then finally closed in September, 1942. Later in 1941 Morecambe was opened as No. 3 Depot."

Grand Hotel, Harrogate now converted to offices
(photo by Alice Gosling, late Autumn 2000)

Appendix II: *Anne Mugridge on WAAF life at RAF Cottesmore*

Through the WAAF. Association I made contact with another WAAF who served at R.A.F. Cottesmore whilst I was also there. Here are a few extracts from Anne Mugridge's letters.

Anne Mugridge (nèe Thain)

I was a volunteer and after two weeks training at Bridgnorth I was posted to R.A.F. Cottesmore, Bomber Command near Oakham in Rutland. My first job was in the Messing Office and at that time our food allowance was 1/6½d per day (about 9p in today's money). This, in fact, gave us three good meals.

On one occasion we had a teleprinter message from the Ministry of Food saying they had traced a certain batch of cornbeef to our station and would we please destroy it as it was not fit for human consumption. Unfortunately we had already eaten it and none of us was any the worse for it. The Warrant Officer in charge of the Mess was a pre-war R.A.F. Regular, Mr. Emmings, who weighed 24½ stone. He had all his clothes made for him and when he got a new uniform I got the job of transferring his polished buttons and sewing on his Warrant Officer's badges etc. The jacket was so heavy—I commented that the pockets looked like shopping bags, to which he replied "Any more of your cheek and I'll put you inside one!". He carried himself very well in spite of the fact he had a piece of shrapnel embedded in the bone of his leg. The villagers from Greetham (over a mile away) told us they always knew when he was on Orderly Officer Duty as they could hear him on Parade. Everyone shuddered when he yelled. However, he was a very fair and understanding person underneath the service rigour. He always told me to obey the rules and used to say it's not worth breaking them because if you are caught you can lose too much. Occasionally he would shout my name from his office window for all to hear, making everyone concerned for me and when I reached his office he would give me his chocolate ration along with the words not to tell anybody else or I wouldn't get anymore and not to eat it all at once.

After one year I was moved to the Document Section in Headquarters but he still bellowed my name out of his window from time to time when he got his chocolate ration. On the last occasion after thanking him and asking how he was he said "I'm alright girl (he always called me girl) but something tells me I must go home this weekend and if the

Commanding Officer doesn't sign my pass I'll go without one". I found this remark very funny coming from him. I left, laughing at him. On the following Monday I was very shocked to hear he had arrived home at 1.00 p.m. on the Saturday and died at 1.30 p.m. I had never been involved in death before and it took some time to get over it. He was kind to me and looked after me as a father would.

In May, 1942 I was leaving the Mess late one afternoon and coming towards me was the Stores Flt/Sgt shouting to me to get in the air-raid shelter. He was running in a zigzag fashion and I stood looking at him thinking he had gone crazy. He reached me and grabbed me, at the same moment I saw the Messerschmitt—we had time to get on the veranda of the Stores building when it passed so low over we could have touched it. The pilot turned his head and looking straight at us, laughed! The Flt/Sgt said "Quick, the Bastard is coming back" and we just had time to run to the other end of the veranda when there he was, spraying the corner we had been standing in with gunfire. He was obviously on reconnaissance as he had no bombs—just firebombs that he dropped on the Sergeant's Mess. Luckily no one was hurt.

Like you I was always on Funeral Parades. The last one they had was after two planes crashed with nine dead. Some went to their homes but I think we took four to the churchyard. It was very emotional and I've always thought of them more so than any of the other incidents I've encountered. After that the orders were no more WAAF on funeral parade.

Sgt Warburton was the only Sgt then, and yes, she was the pleasant large lady—firm but always had time to talk to you and help you when she could—a cut above the others. She was the only decent Sgt we had. She was made a F/Sgt and when we moved to Market Harborough she was posted to the Middle East.

Do I remember Blands buses! The last one from Oakham—airmen in first, then a WAAF on every knee, and those left over filled the luggage racks and the gangway. I can't remember them ever breaking down.

Your 'Pyjamas and the Tin Hat' made me laugh and reminded me of our navy blue pure wool knickers. My oldest sister was in the A.T.S. and, of course, had the same best quality Smedley's knickers in khaki. We both sent them home to Mother with strict instructions that if she got a telegram from us she must post them back as we were due for a kit inspection. Needless to say she would send us the wrong colour and though we told her, when they wore out, if she would let us have them we would exchange them for a new pair—being a very thrifty Scot she considered this to be very extravagant and would cut up one pair to patch the other—to try and tell her we would be in trouble for having a pair of knickers short—well she thought we were just being childish.

My Dad found all this very amusing as he had been in the Army and knew we were telling the truth. The final straw to end this tale was when war finished and the knickers wore out, Mother found she was too cold in the thinner, prettier ones and he had to buy Smedleys which were expensive, so Dorothy and I were blamed for him having to waste such a lot of money. We assured her she was lucky as she could now buy them in white or pink.

Our first billets were in the Officers' houses next to the Officers' Mess, and yes, there would have been over 200 of us by June 1942, as every month there was approximately another 20.

Do you remember Jack Nathan and his Band? We had great dance nights with him. Camp Dances were held in the Mens' NAAFI next to the Mess. They could remove the partitions and make it into a really large Hall (NAAFI and Mess) together. Concerts, too, were held in this way and films.

Appendix III: *Exam Papers*

These are copies of my Clerk (General Duties) exam papers which I took. Only one is dated—29th June, 1941. When I enlisted I was an Airwoman 2nd class. The above paper would have been taken so that I could become an Airwoman 1st class.

According to Bob Owen's letter of 4th July, 1943 I had just been promoted to the rank of Leading Aircraftwoman with 4d. per day increase in pay.

I now have no idea which exam is which—or if any were for my Cpl exams in August, 1944. The one thing I do know for sure is that I wonder how I managed to answer them so successfully—I never had to do any re-takes!

LOCAL TRADE TEST BOARD
'A' PAPER

Time allowed - 3 hours.
All questions are to be answered:-

(i)   Write an application for your discharge from the Service to take up work of National Importance.
(ii) Complete the attached Form 200 in respect of yourself.
(iii) Compare the types of index you know.
(iv) What is the meaning of the following Service and Non-Service abbreviations:-
      J.A.G. R.A.F.SP. P.AM.O. C.M.C. S.P.S.O. ad.lib., ipso facto S.M.O., A.O.C. in C. M.A.F.L.
(v)   Draft a letter to Air Ministry for your Commanding Officer's signature stating his

idea of the organisation of an O.T.U.

Written Paper – Clerk G.D. – 'B' PAPER

TIME ALLOWED - THREE HOURS

10 marks each question

1. What are the following forms:-

    P. 182   :   F.96   :   F.143   :

    F421   :

    P. 348   :   F.48   :   F.658   :

    F.514   :

    P.125   :   :   F.12   :

2. An aircraft apprentice enlisted on 1.1.30, he attained the age of 18 on 1.1.32, he passed out from the training establishment on 6.1.33 - when was he due for the award of his first Good Conduct Badge. Only entry on his conducts sheets - forfeiture of one days pay for absence.

3. In what instances may free Railway Warrants be issued.

4. What action is taken when a Commanding Officer considers that an airman is inefficient in his trade.

5. Explain:-

    (a) How secret and confidential correspondence is received in a unit.

    (b) How secret and confidential correspondence is despatched from a Unit.

6. (a) When is an Airman's character assessed.

    (b) When is an assessment of an Airman's trade proficiency made.

7. What leave can an airman have and what amounts.

8. Give the titles of the following publications:-

    A.P.A   958:   A.P. 804:   A.P. 1112:

    A.P. 830, Vol. I

9. What are the qualifications governing the award of the Long Service and Good Conduct medal.

10. State the amounts an airman can be fined for drunkenness.

LOCAL TRADE TEST BOARD - CLERKS G.D.

'B' PAPER

Time allowed - 3 hours

All questions to be answered

(i)   (a) For what purpose are Personnel Occurrence Reports (Airmen) prepared and distributed.

      (b) Give example entries under the following headings, preparing and setting out a P.O.R. in the correct form and sequence, for airmen

      (i)   Punishment.

      (ii) Discharge (Medical).

(iii)   Posting.

(iv)   Birth.

(v)   Absence without leave.

(ii)   (a) Give all authorities under which the following promotions or appointments may be effected.

Temporary Corporal, Acting Corporal,

Temporary Flight Sergeant, Acting Warrant Officer

(b) Give short account of the present rules governing the re-classification of A.C.H. Group V trades, other than Drivers M.T., Parachute Packers, Telephone Operators, Gunner, Service Police.

(iii)   Give a short account of the procedure adopted on the discharge of an airman on appointment to a Temporary Commission.

Note:-   Discharge action only required.

(iv)   Compile an Officer's P.O.R. showing entries under the following headings:

Acting Promotions. (appointing and converting G.D. Branch and any other branch) 'C'   'E' (i)   'E' (ii)   'E' (iii)   'H' 'J' 'M'.

(v)   (a)   Describe briefly the contents of the Air Force List.

(b)   What is the outfit allowance allowed by the Air Ministry for a newly commissioned officer.

(c)   Name eight branches of the R.A.F.

(d)   Give the titles of the following forms: 381, 1443, 506, 373, 274, 1707, 78

(e)   Who is the C. in C. Bomber Command.

(f) Indicate what action is taken for newly commissioned officer on arrival at his joining unit.

(g) To what do the following refer:-

A.M.O. A.913/40, A.366/40, K.R. & A.C.I. 867, A.P.826

(vi) Write a letter to Air Ministry notifying the change of address of the next of kin of an officer

(vii) Compile a D.R.O. giving the following:-

(i) Black-Out, (ii) Duties, (iii) Water supply economy

(iv) Availability of Savings Stamps on a Unit Pay Parade

(v) Court of Inquiry into the loss of a Revolver

(viii) An airman enlists on 2.1.36, and on 3.4.36, he is awarded 14 days C.C. and forfeiture of one days pay. On 3.4.38 he is fined 3/- for drunkenness. When is this airman awarded a Good Conduct Badge.

(ix) What are the filing systems in general use in the Royal Air Force. Describe one in detail.

(x) An airman applies for a commission in the A. & S. D. Branch. Assuming he fulfils all necessary conditions, and enlisted on 5.9.39, state the action taken by the Unit in disposing of this application.

Written Paper - Clerks G.D.   **'A' PAPER**

TIME ALLOWED - THREE HOURS 10 marks each question

1. Prepare a Standing Order setting out the duties for the Duty Clerk.

2. Give a short account of your duties as Clerk in the Department where you are employed.

3. Name four Non-Public Accounts.

4. Prepare a Daily Routine Order showing an Order regarding a Court of Enquiry over a M.T. Accident.

5. State from what source Railway Warrants are obtainable.

   What steps are taken for their safe custody.

6. State the equivalent rank in the Royal Air Force of the following:-

NAVY	ARMY
Admiral	General
Lieutenant	Major
	Brigadier

7. State the names of the Commands of the R.A.F.

8. Complete the attached Form 551.

9. Define the following terms:-

   MSS: : A.I.D. : A.M.F.S. : A.O.C.-in-C. : D.D. :
   P.S.I. : R.A.F.O. : P.M.C. : E.G.M.

10. What are the purposes of:-

    (a) Daily Routine Orders

    (b) P.O.R's

LOCAL TRADE TEST BOARD - CLERKS GENERAL DUTIES
29th JUNE, 1941